To

TINA

With
All
Best
Wishes

DonEric

ABBEYFIELD
    SOCIETY
AUGUST 2007

From Dust to Flowers

Also by the same author

FEAST OF EXPECTANCY

THE PAINTER

From Dust to Flowers
A Day in the Life of Rural Mexico

A Narrative Prose Poem

Don Eric Carroll

Illustrated by Tess Stone

ROS
Ruadh

First edition published in 1998 by
Ros Ruadh
P.O.Box 812, Windsor, Berkshire, SL4 5XH

ISBN 1 900597 02 0

British Library Cataloguing-in-Publication Data.
A catalogue record for this book is available from the British Library.

Set in " Times New Roman"; printed on Kestrel Cream,cover in Strathmore
Americana Nantucket Ivory.

Printed by Lavenham Press Ltd. Lavenham, Suffolk.

To my grandsons

Dominic Ricardo
and
Carlo Luigi

Foreword

When I first read the typescript I had no idea of what to
expect, knowing nothing about the author or Mexico. After the
first reading,I knew that I was holding in my hands a book
which would stay in my mind for a long time - *Pancho* had
entered my conciousness, as had the village of *San Angelo del
Castillo,* the two ranches and the *Ramos* family.
*"FROM DUST TO FLOWERS: A Day in the Life of Rural
Mexico"* is as precisely descriptive as the sub-title "a narrative
prose poem ". This is a unique read. The pages offer a slim
track of words which look like poetry and prose,they are easy
to read, not dense, yet have the resonance and self-awareness
of poetry.Like a novel with the boring bits taken out, like lying
in bed being read to, the rhythm and sensuousness of the story
is there, but the more prosaic details are mercifully withheld !
And sensuous this book is ,above all.

It is visual, but it also carries the skin feeling of heat and flies,
the rich and varying smells, the sounds and what one can only
call the feeling of Mexico. It is the story of childish hope, a
difficult birth, a sordid and messy death, old age, a family
holding together despite the odds, and the coming of a violent
and long awaited but nonetheless unexpected salvation.
The narrative begins when two sisters waken.The peace of the
sunny room, the innocence and the nascent sexuality of the
girls, the delicious and irresponsible pause of the children
between waking and engaging with the rest of the family are
captured in minutely detailed language which seems to survey
with the girls' eyes the present moment with -
> "dust motes floating and swirling
> in shifting lemon rays."

Once the girls are awake and laughing uncontrollably, the
book's day is fully launched. The boy comes home from the

fields with his dog, the family eats breakfast together, the girls go to market, a goat is slaughtered, and around these rough, sensual people, all the time, there is a sense of powerful and inexorable natural forces.The sun beats and dries, the wind stirs, blood pumps, flies buzz and invade everything, the heat is intolerable, but the darkness stinks.

As I read this beautiful book and re-read it, I am struck more and more by its paradox. The lives of the people depicted are real and hard.They are drawn from life. But the danger and dirt, the discomfort and paucity of their lives is overwhelmingly compensated by the vibrant richness of every minute of their day. This becomes clearest in the penultimate section when a family supper is held to celebrate....*well* , to
celebrate being alive and being able to enjoy it. It is a great feast but a humble occasion. There is dancing and drunkenness and delicious food, but this is a regular event for the *Ramos* family, and the floorshow is provided as much by the setting sun as by the old man dancing with the young girl.

It is hard to give the true flavour of this powerful book because it is distilled out of true and carefully observed experience. Like the paintings of *Diego Rivera* it celebrates the mundane and the ordinary. In sensuous detail that is never obsessive, but always precise to the extent of being shocking, we the readers are brought through the prose poetry into a world of drought-burdened peasantry, recalcitrant domestic animals, steaming food, dust, dust, and eventually in a sudden and miraculous denouement, *flowers* !
Read *From Dust to Flowers*, read it slowly and enjoy it. It will remind you that the only deadly things in life are comfort, ease, safety and the predictable.
It will also make you long to go to rural Mexico!

Nicholas W Bayley
Reading 1997

Contents

Book One

"Morning"

PART 1

The sun rose
out of the Atlantic
and seared its mark
in the clear
     Mexican sky.

     Gradually
it left the castellated
     rim
of the eastern *cordillera,*
s   p   r   e   a   d   i   n   g
golden light
over the vast expanse
of the *meseta*
- the high central plateau -
with its arid
blasted landscape
of tawny hills
and tumbled fissures
of stark
     desolate
        ravines.
The sun's fast growing heat
and harsh light
swallowed shreds of mist
hugging the shallow agricultural valleys.
Soon the heat will come on
and the dust rise.

             Situated
in one of these valleys,
lying central of the broad basin
of the meseta,
is the *pueblo*
of *San Angelo del Castillo*.
At the north end of the valley
stands a 17th century monastery
with a fortlike exterior
of whitewashed crenellated walls.
This ancient building
had been converted
- so it was said -
converted to military barracks
for the soldiers
      of Ferdinand Maximilian,
then used as a federal grain warehouse,
and finally abandoned.
             During
the tulmultuous era
of the post - *Conquistadors*,
the monastery
spawned the tiny village,
the village of San Angelo
- the adjunct 'del Castillo '
added a century later.

The deep morning stillness
                    melted
into a vibrancy of myriad sounds
over the humble adobe huts
in the pueblo,
the village of San Angelo.

A burst of birdsong
spilled out
from the scattered beefwood trees
and echoed among the cattail rushes
·and tall stands of reed grass
along the river bank
threading the valley floor.
Thin voices of insects
cried in the air
and a whispering of wind
- fil - ter - ed -
through short ranks
of wavering
        pale gold
                grasses.
Domestic animals and peasants
                alike
stirred from the simple
        comfort of reed debris
and straw woven mats,
their bodies
        redolent of dull
                warmth,
like early morning hearth ash.

Ah, rise up Mexico !
Speak to us of your heat
and dusty winds,
your heat and flies,
flies and smells and heat.

        The pueblo
of San Angelo and *redonda*
(that is, the surrounding district)
        portrayed
a composition of mosaic earthcolours;
sienna tiling on the hut roofs,
struck copper red now

by shafts of sunlight
driving between tall organ cactus;
beige wattled fencing
forming the corral boundaries,
the corrals enclosing
rust-brown cattle
trampling docilely
in a shredded crispness
of yellow-ochre ground straw.
The furrowed *milpas*,
                    parching
from a long dry season,
                    presented
dark-brown faces to the sun,
absorbing its brightness
        and fierce rays.
The fields stretched
flat and rectangularly
to a dun-coloured sand river bank.
And beyond the river
- at this time of year
        little more
than a rock -cobbled stream -
rugged hills flanked the valley,
throwing back heat shimmerings
of bronze
        and sepia
            and gold.
                The southern area
was dominated by a steep sloped
                hill
beautifully carved by nature
into the shape of a woman's
                    breast.

The illusion was heightened
by a long-derelict chapel
stood at the summit
like an erect nipple.

This notable landmark was given
 the ancient Chichimecan name of
' The Hill That Invites ',
and so it was no coincidence
that the male members
of the pueblo community
should call it
        Breast Hill.

                Suddenly,
as if coming up
from out of the earth,
there appeared several
        tlacololeros
on the hillsides.
These sombreroed men
bent their backs,
hands and *machetes*
        scrabbling
to clear rocks and stubble
and decayed *maguey* plants
from their meagre plots,
the sun on their backs
and the dust in their eyes.
And in the fields
strode columns of milperos,
in single file and evenly spaced
        like birds
        on a telegraph wire,
their feet raising dust
in the rutted hollows
of irrigation trenches.

In the pueblo, too,
people were out and about,
        mainly women,
wearing blue-grey *rebozos*
of finely woven thread,
followed by a scampering
    of dark-faced
    ragged children
            and mongrel dogs.

        A record
played on a wind-up Victrola
and the music flowed
    with a tinny timbre
    from the brass
        flaring horn,
f l o o d i n g
the valley with its sound.
For the duration of any day
        and well into the night
this music would be heard
by the peasants in the valley.

        The chapel bell pealed
in competition with the music,
the music from the old phonograph.
And so the bell rang,
its liquid notes poured
    munificently
    across the land.

Roosters crowed
    belligerently
    energetically,
and dogs barked
and cattle roared and bellowed

in a feverish melody of madness
as they were driven out
    to pasture
by barefooted boys
      throwing stones
      and wielding sticks.

And the heat came on
and the dust rose
and San Angelo del Castillo
      exploded alive
      to another day.

PART 2

       Some little distance
west of the sensually contoured hill
    topped by the chapel,
stood, sentinel-wise, a solitary hut,
cane-walled and windowless.
This modest structure was set back
from a winding goat track
and afforded a broad view
of the valley's slightly curved length.
In this hut on the hill rise
a lone man got up
    without undue reluctance
from his frayed-edged *petate*.
He rolled up the tule reed mat
and stood it in a corner.
He had slept fully clothed
    in a grubby-grey shirt
    and old-styled *calzones*
    of coarse cotton cloth,
tied with rope at the waist and ankles.

He yawned   w   i   d   e   l   y
and abstractedly scratched himself
    under his armpits
    and around the base
    of his spine.
Then he slipped dusty, calloused feet
in *huaraches*-the poor man's sandals,
crudely cut from old automobile tyres -
and he stamped into them
on the hard-packed earthen floor.
    He was a short man,
broad in the shoulders and chunkily built,
as if roughly chiseled from a block
    of hard-grained wood.

He was bandy-legged like a horseman
and walked with a lopsided gait.
A history of hardship was plainly scrawled
over his dark bronze beaten features,
his left cheek marred
by a livid downward running scar,
giving him a wild savage brigand look.
This was offset to a point
by the continual humorous sparkle
                    in his eyes,
which were expressive and milky-blue,
the blue of a tropical sea
    at first light of dawn.
But the most striking aspect
    of his appearance
was the bristled tuft of ginger hair
                    on his skull,
looking rather like
    what a horse would snap
        from a hay-rack.
The local villagers,
with that sharp peasant sense
of perception of things
pertaining to the earth,
sometimes called him *Mazorca*.
    (Corncob)
His real name was
    Francisco Medina Ramírez.
    Or 'Pancho', to his friends.

        Pancho
knuckled the sleep from his eyes,
then pulled absently
at his bushy down-sweeping moustache,
gazing meditatively
        at his familiar surrounds.
The tiny one-roomed hut
appeared Spartan to an extreme.

24

Light, filtered through chinks
        in the cane-stalked walls,
exposed Pancho's only material wealth,
        or the lack of it.
        On one side,
before a smoke-blackened wall,
stood a low stone hearth,
a pile of silver-white ash
        cool in the bowl.
Where Pancho slept,
a half full sack of mouldy corn
leaned against the wall,
in company with a clay water jar,
its top protected
        by a round wooden board
        with a corncob handle.
The opposite side was adorned
        with nothing more
than a coarsely woven *sarape*
        and a straw *sombrero*
        hung on a nail,
and a wooden crate of dusty,
        undefinable junk.
Above, at a normal man's height,
was grouped a trio of earthenware pots,
handles roped and hung on a meathook
        in the main log beam.
        There was no sign
of knick-knacks or pictures or anything
        that could be termed superfluous,
but on the slatted clapboard door
        was pasted long ago
the front page of a newspaper,
flyblown and parchment-brown with age.
Now faded print told of the assassination
        of President Obregón
and the dissolving of the *Confederación*

Regional de Obreros Mexicanos,
events that had occured
back in Pancho's early years.

It was, quite evidently,
a very poor man's dwelling,
like many another in this cruel,
this heat-burdened, dust-laden,
fly-ridden tortured savage land.

At this moment
Pancho's eyes fell on the empty hearth.
Wood was needed for a fire
in order to heat a breakfast dish
                of corn gruel.

"*Oye*, now stop a bit, you,"
            said Pancho to himself,
            as old men do when living alone,
"you'll be wanting some fire here
if you're going to stuff your face,
and that's a fact. Hmm, true enough."
And Pancho looked again at the hearth.
"Well move yourself *hombre*,
            it's a working day.
            Újule ! as it always is
            for the likes of you."
And Pancho gimped out into the sunshine
blinking at the blinding light,
gimped round to a woodpile in the shade
            at the rear of his little hut.

        Brown-mottled hands
drove into the loosely stacked wood,
fingers groping for twigs.
And in the process of his groping
dislodged a scorpion hidden there,
which fell in a litter of woodchips

on the hardtrodden ground.
Pancho's keen eyes caught it instantly,
for it was all of half a hand long.

       "Ha!" said Pancho
in a gravelled voice and contemptuous tone.
"Is it you to live on my property, then ?
No, damn you, you're not welcome here.
           On my property ! Hmn..umm - m."
And with the end of a log Pancho ground
the creature into the earth, into the dust.
And the scorpion's stinger strummed
and a bubble of viscous fluid oozed
               from its distal end.
"Ha!" repeated Pancho in the same
contemptuous sort of tone; and,
having gathered up a supply of wood,
    he gimped back indoors.

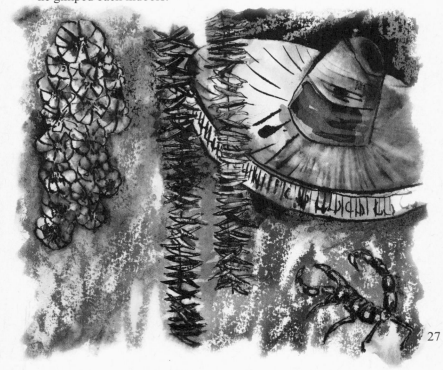

PART 3

A time later,
Pancho's steady gaze swept over
the heat shimmered land in a careful survey,
    then stopped sunwards
    at a distorted blob of life
    approaching from the hilltop.
He thumbed his eye socket and looked again,
fastening his pale blue eyes on a man
    astride the crupper
    of a lightly laden
    but greatly emaciated
    burro-or donkey -
with a young woman following
    a few paces behind.

Nearer now,
the skinny burro minced on awkward legs
as it followed the stony goat track,
    stiffening its forequarters
    on a downward dip in shadow.
Its hooves clipped the stones
    and milled the earth crust,
    and the crust crumbled,
        turned to dust.
It jibbed to a sudden halt,
straddled limbs trembling,
right in front of Pancho's hut.

Pancho waved a friendly hand
in greeting to the strangers,
with welcoming acceptance of some much
needed company to ease his
    habitual desolate loneliness,
and casually taking in the potware
strung broadside on the beast,
clattering tinnily by scraggy flanks.

The man slid swiftly and effortlessly
over the rump of his beast
in that manner peculiar to the Mexican *campesino*,
and rubbed the palms of his sweaty hands
    down patched pants.
The woman took the rope rein
    without a word
    and quietly led the burro
    to the scant shade
    of a nearby scrub tree.

"*Buenos días!* Good morning!" said Pancho,
    with obvious enthusiasm,
in his graveled, rasping tone of voice,
one hand extended as he loped forward
and the other courteously lifting
    his sombrero clear from his head.
And the stranger, his face powdered
    with fine orange dust,
showed an open dirt-grimed palm.
"Sit yourself!" said Pancho,
offering the dubious comfort
of a matted cob of earth
stuck up in the ground
like a giant hairy wart.
While Pancho squatted nimbly on his hunkers
    before the stranger
and began to roll gently forward and back
    on his toes and heels.

"*Qué va!* it's a melter today, hombre,
    and no mistake,"
he opened up good-humouredly,
the weathered lines on his face
    dancing as he spoke.

30

"Here we are in the second July week,
fields cleared of stone and ready
for the planting and all that.
And-well then, what's happened
        to our raining season ?
Did we get one last year ?
How much rain did we see last year ?
Why.enough to wash the face
        of a piddling cucaracha.
        Eh, hombre ? Damn right.
Raining season my sweet arse !"
And Pancho laughed uproariously.

The stranger's features,
thickly streaked with dust and sweat,
smiled hesitantly and shyly;
and Pancho nodded with a crafty wink,
as though to say: "Why yes, we are men
                and know the score."
Then a brief pregnant silence followed
as the two men openly appraised each other,
like a dog sniffing another,
while the hot malignant sun
        flared down on them.

    "Tell me, hombre,"
 Pancho began again presently,
his hand pulling at his moustache
        and rocking on his heels,
"where are you come from
        and where do you go ?
I trust Saint Anthony is with you."
"By La Cruz del Palma, *señor*,"
The stranger returned briefly.

"Ah, La Cruz, eh. *Qué bueno*, that's good.
And where is it you go ?"
"The town. The big town."
"*Sí* ? The big town, eh ?"
Pancho echoed, in his gruff, husky voice,
gazing steadily into the man's
        coffee-brown eyes.
"The market, señor,"
the man expanded further.
" To be sure,the market.
Umm-m. Qué bueno, qué bueno."
Pancho automatically and instinctively
rippled a hand in front of him
to scatter a cloud of flies.
"I have pots to sell,"
the stranger resumed,
indicating the laden donkey
with a motion of his arm.
"So I see, and there they are,"
said Pancho, and gave the stranger

        a knowing wink.

Pancho turned slightly to one side
and blew his nose between his fingers
to clear the dust from there, then said
        inquisitively and meaningly:
"You came by way of *el castillo*,
        the castle, eh ?"
looking straight at the man.
The stranger nodded.
"Then," Pancho pursued
        matter-of-factly now,
"you must have come by Camacho's *hacienda*."
And the stranger screwed up his face
        in puzzlement
and rubbed a hand over his jaw.

"The young *don* I'm speaking of,"
         rasped Pancho,
"don Cesar Camacho,
who runs the cattle ranch over that way,"
·and Pancho pointed a stubby finger
      to the northwest.
"Ah, him," the stranger said,
understanding at last.
"Sí, that one," said Pancho
         with a good-natured grin.
Pancho rocked to and fro on his heels,
and thought to himself :
He doesn't know who I mean, I'll bet,
and the stranger rubbed his jaw.
"The *ranchero*," he said.
"A cousin of mine worked for him
for a time-let's see now -
some seventeen years ago,
         I think, or thereabouts,"
and he dropped his hand and rubbed a knee.
"That'll be don Cesar the elder
         you're thinking on," Pancho said,
and gave the stranger a curious look.
"Did you know him ?" he grated.
"No," the man drawled slowly
               and thoughtfully,
"but my cousin did,
because he worked for him, this Camacho."
The stranger lifted his sombrero
         as though he were embarrassed;
and then, on a sudden impulse,
he finger scissored his sweat-dampened hair.
Pancho chuckled throatily,
amused at something or another, and said :
"He was a regular original that one !"
"The ranchero fellow ?" asked the stranger,
brown eyes lighting up with interest.

"Sí, yes, hombre," Pancho grinned,
stroking the ends of his moustache.
"He's dead now, is he ?" asked the stranger.
"Sí, the don, he took himself off a long time back,"
and Pancho slapped his thigh with high satisfaction.
The stranger thrust his sombrero
      back on his skull,
leaned forward and rested elbows on his knees.
Pancho's eyes strayed upward
and caught on a hawk in the high clear air,
far in the distance and moving so slow
that it appeared as if pinned
to the cerulean backdrop of the sky.
Then Pancho dropped his gaze
and turned to look at the stranger,
and the milkspot pigments
      in the blue of his eyes
seemed to twinkle with secret amusement.

Pancho grinned at him with natural good humour
and went on at last,
his voice graveled and grating,
as though he had a mouthful of grit
      tearing at his vocal chords.
"You see, hombre," he said, "I worked for him too,
      this Cesar Camacho....."
And the stranger nodded and raised an eyebrow.
He patted his kneecaps,
then rubbed a hand down one shin.
Pancho toed a pebble in the dust,
paused to think what he might say,
glancing with a somewhat accusing eye
at the hills and the distant mountains
      shivering in a heat haze.
A hot wind blew and the dust hung heavy
in the dessicated air,
almost with shape and feature,
      as an apparition.
"Well, I'll tell you...."
34

PART 4

"Aye qué caray hombre,
I worked for this don Cesar long before
            your cousin did,"
Pancho began conversationally,
grinning widely and savagely at the stranger.
He continually rocked back and forth
on his heels as he spoke.
"The don, he found me in a *cantina*
in the mining town of Zacatecas - You know it ?"
and the stranger knowing it, nodded.
"Újule ! drunk and stupid as an *indio*
        I was on *mezcal*,
in them days before the don went and hired me.
For I was newly wed then, you see,
and that took some getting used to -
though she's been long dead,
may her soul rest in peace,"
and Pancho made the sign of the cross,
his face for a moment clouding over.
He squinted his eyes upward at the ocean of sunlight,
and a kind of peace was reflected in those eyes
as they watched the high wind's hand
shape a solitary streak of cloud
        into pillowlike puffs of smoke.

Pancho wet his lips with his tongue,
        and went on :
"Sí, in those days I was nought
but a bullheaded drunken fool,
though a fine herdsman and known
        in all the northern states, *carajo* !
Ah, the weeks I spent on horseback,
chaffing my arse to the raw.
I drove cattle clear across
that great Chihuahuan desert

and on through to the banks
    of the Rio Bravo.
Ayí! I was as good as a Paracho guitar,"
    Pancho boasted.
and his eye lines crinkled with amusement
and tiny particles of dust
ran down his swarthy cheeks.

He shook his head,
and hawked and spat in the dust.
    "No, look, hombre,"
he continued in that incredibly dry,
husky, rasping tone of voice,
as if he were chewing fine gravel,
and thrusting a finger at the scar on his cheek,
"See this mark ? Well, then,
it was done by a steer's horn
when I worked in Durango,
oh years and years ago,"
wagging a finger in front of his face.
"He was a heavy lumbering beast and all,
    a real *cabrón*, a *chingon chingon*.
But I'll say this for that
two-horned old *cabrone*,
he could move as fast as a jackrabbit
    with an ant up its arse."
Pancho's finger hovered in the air.
"He ripped my best goatskin chaps
and pinched my cheek here a little bit,
    do you see it ?"
tapping the ridge of the scar
with the pad of his finger.

Pancho dropped his hand
    to his knee and sighed.
"Then this don Cesar came along
and he found me in Zacatecas.

Por la Santísima,
he'd heard of my reputation
and knew my name as well.
            Pancho Ramirez !
Only, some people call me Corncob,
on account of this here, you see ?"
and he lifted his sombrero fully from his head
to display his spiked ginger hair,
and wiped his brow with the back of his hand,
and his humorous eyes seemed to say
"Well, what's in a crop of hair anyhow !"

He clicked his teeth and winked
a merry eye at the stranger,
then clapped his sombrero
back where it belonged.
" 'Pancho,' says this hombre,
I'd like a word or two with you.'
'Well,here I am !' I says to him.
'But later,' says he, the don,
and eyeing me up and down
like I was a horse for sale.
'When you're good and sober, Pancho.
You come and see me later, eh?'
And he was right, you see,
for I was so drunk I put my foot
        in a damned spittoon!
And that was that. Mm-m, he hired me
        there in Zacatecas.
Sí, and on that very next day
I was on my way to Juarez
with foul-stinking cattle
throwing up the dust and shit.
Chingada, I rode with the don
for what must have been weeks on end,
over the plains from ranch to ranch,
buying and selling, chaffering and arguing,

selecting horses to breed -
to sell to the military. Hmm.
Over the high *sierras*
and across the empty grazing plains,
where you wouln't meet another human soul
except maybe once in a couple of weeks.
And he brought me back here to San Angelo
and the *hacienda* over that way a bit,"
with a quick nod of his head.
"And I lived in the stables
with them fine sorrels and bays
and a smart-looking appaloosa filly.
      Ay chócala !
Then I sent word for my little wife
to come down and join me
- for she was living with her mother
      in Gomez Palacio -
and we were given a room of our own
at the end of the stables."

Pancho scraped the heel of his huarache
      through deep silky dust.
He worked his cheeks and jaw for a while,
then turned his head and spat
      neatly on the ground.
There was a high hum of flies
busy about withered gorsebrush
lining the rock-studded goat track.
Pancho gazed off into the shimmering distance,
his eyes seemingly smiling
as they squinted narrowly at the hot sunlight.
He rolled his jaws some more,
as though he were eating a meal.
He turned abruptly then
and faced the stranger.

"The don came out ahead with his horses,"
he went on, in husky mournful tones,
"but not so my little wife
and the *muchachas* I gave her.
O Dios mío, three all told
and sweet little darlings
　　　　they were too.
And each of them died of this
or died of that
before they could even walk
on their own two feet.
　　　　　Carambas !
it was the dying of the little ones
that killed her off too, you understand ?
May they rest in some peace now,"
and Pancho crossed himself jerkily.
"We had a room all to our own,
but a small room you might say,
for we were tight like chillies
　　　　in a pickle jar."

　　　Pancho paused
and licked his dust-dry lips.
He looked over the barren wasteland hills,
at scattered colonies of blue-green maguey plants,
at the sun-scarred bush and scrub,
and the air shimmer under the sun's heat.
His eyes rested for a time on the pueblo
and the fields in the valley.
At length, he turned his chunky frame
and glanced at the stranger, then said :
"Well, don Cesar, he treated me well
enough in those early years.
But I don't work for him or his son no more.
I work now, at least sometimes, for the Ramos family.
Down near those trees there by the river,"
indicating terraced foliage of a beech wood
stepping up from the riverbank opposite the pueblo.

"Well hombre, somewhere in that wood
is where the Ramos family live.
A small ranch, you might say.
Ay look there, hombre, you can see the cornstore,
red-tiled and proper you'll appreciate.
They have orchards too, the Ramos people,
and raise hogs and chickens of course."
Pancho fingered his moustache
and rocked slightly on his heels.
The two men were silent for a spell,
each with his own thoughts.
They listened to the noises of the land.
A drone of insects worried the sun-scoured air,
roving in clouds over brown nopal cactus
                    and twisted gorsebush.
 A cock crowed in the pueblo,
and a donkey loudly brayed
in a field of alfalfa in the valley.
The phonograph music drifted to them
        pleasantly, dreamily ;
and it seemed as if it were coming
out of the very earth of the hills.
The chapel bell pealed from the white-washed,
        sun-washed bell-tower,
making hollow oscillations which travelled
in echoing waves through the stinging
        dust-sifted air.
                    Presently, the stranger
politely coughed to attract Pancho's attention,
rubbing and kneading the thin stretch
of muscle over his kneecaps.
And then he stood abruptly
and wiped his palms against dusty pants.
"I must be off, señor," he said.
And Pancho jumped instantly to his feet
with surprising alacrity.
"Well, you're on your way then, eh?"
said Pancho, an element of disbelief

in the tone of his voice,
as if the stranger was there
merely for Pancho's pleasure.
"Sí, I must," the man said,
and he went to shake Pancho by the hand,
with the customary politeness
        of the Mexican campesino.

        Moments later,
the man took the rein from his wife's hand
and led the burro down the track
which wound away round the hill.
The young woman followed submissively
behind her husband as before,
her rather dainty feet picking their way
carefully over sharp, loose rocks.
And once more Pancho was reminded of a woman
he had known and loved and cherished.
He was in fact thinking of his long dead wife.

Pancho regretfully watched them go,
tugging fiercely at his moustache,
a wreath of flies busy about him.
He would visit the Ramos family today,
        he promised himself,
as indeed he had promised the family,
but had forgotten he had done so.

The couple disappeared from his view
        behind a bluff,
and he wheeled resolutely on his heels.
Dust-devils pirouetted across the goat track,
and insects buzzed angrily
in the smother of dust about Pancho.
And the wind blew hotly
and the heat hammered
        down on the land.

PART 5

"Ruth ?"
The child's voice was low, sweet,
      and tenderly melodious.
There was a soft rustle of a bedsheet
as the child turned over
with a quick fluid movement.
She leaned on one elbow,
her small chin cupped in her hand,
and gazed with wide eyes at her elder sister,
who was half curled and sleeping soundly
      beside her.

"Ruth !"
The intonation of the voice was now urgent
with childish impatience.
Bright morning sunshine streamed
through a tiny one-paned window,
the beam of light probing a red brick floor,
dust motes floating and swirling
      in shifting lemon rays.
A fly alighted on the sleeping girl's cheek,
and her cheek twitched and her lips
      appeared to form a brief smile.
The child saw the movement
      and giggled to herself,
then immediately suppressed it.

"R - Rutí !"
The girl slept on serenely,
perhaps subliminally entranced in the last
of the night's cycle of wondrous dreams
      with which the young are blessed.
The mellow light in the room
richly enhanced her lovely olive skin
      as she slept on.

The child's voice became persistent :
"Ruth, are you awake ?"
and she shook the smoothly rounded
shoulder of her sister.
The girl stirred restively a moment,
her hands locked in the valley
of her slightly swelling thighs.
Her small, budlike breasts rose
and fell evenly, and her long, glossy hair
was unbound and spilled over a pillow.
She smiled in her sleep,
a soft and gentle smile,
showing perfectly even, pearly-white teeth.

The child giggled again.
"So, you're only pretending,"
she whispered with amusement,
and her warm honeyed breath
caressed the other's cheek
as she leaned over her.
"Well, I'm asleep too !"
she declared in a fierce whisper,
and with that she turned
and dived under the bedsheet,
burrowing to the bottom of the bed
        like a squirrel.
She lay there rigid and expectant,
her breath flowing between open teeth
in one long, strained exhalation.

        Ruth half awakened.
"Julia ?" she said softly. "Julia, are you up ?"
and there was no answer.
Fully aroused now, Ruth uncurled
        and stretched luxuriously.
She threw back the sheet to her waist,
and her hands explored under the shift,and felt
the rich warm softness of her slender body.

Her mind marvelled at the silk
smoothness of her skin
which was suffused with bed warmth.
Her hands moved on up to her small breasts
and she squeezed them tentatively,
with the brief surge of delight and pride
of one recently out of childhood
yet still very much a child.
Her finger crept up and touched her throat,
and she released her breath
        in a prolonged sigh.

"Julia," she said langourously,
"it's time to be up, don't you think ?"
"No it isn't then,"
came the muffled reply
from the wriggling mound at her feet,
"because I'm still fast asleep
and you're disturbing my dream."

Ruth moved her leg sideways and her toes
found warm, soft, vibrant flesh.
"Don't !"
"What's your dream about ?"
"You really want to know ?"
"Why yes, what is it, tell me !"
Julia tittered, her little body shaking.
She fidgeted and tossed and turned,
and the sheet peeled off the bed
        in a sliding wave.
She goggled her eyes and poked out the tip
of her tongue at her sister.
"There !" she cried,
"the dream went away with the *nahual*,"
and Julia threw back her head and laughed,
a peal of merriment so spontaneously
        contagious and appealing

that it forced Ruth, not unnaturally
to also burst out in laughter.
For a moment Julia was unable
to control her laughter,
and her two braids swung
like puppets on a string.
At last she stopped and managed
     to compose herself.
She drew up her slim legs
and clasped hands about her knees,
and her face was filled with a happy radiance,
     innocent and utterly carefree.
She wriggled and squirmed her small frame
in order to get herself comfortable.
She then cast a glance at her sister
with what can only be described as candid eyes.
The pair of them were obviously enjoying
the private coziness of their little room ;
and knowing, without apparently a sense of guilt,
that other members of the Ramos family
were bustling industriously with many chores.

Julia soon grew restive,
as children usually are first thing of a morning.
She put a finger to her lips
and secretively whispered :
"I'm going to see what's going on,"
and she swung lithely from the bed,
a tender lemon light falling on her oval face.
She skipped lightly to the tiny window
and peeked through the dust streaked glass
and her eyes glittered with impish mischief
as they roved fleetingly over the yard
     of the busy farmstead.
"*Mamá* looks pleased with herself....."

PART 6

      Woodsmoke billowed up
in great clouds from a stone hearth
under the kitchen lean-to across the yard,
and a huge black cauldron sat
like an ancient Indian idol
on the flames of the kitchen fire.
The supporting beams of the lean-to
were thick-limbed logs of beefwood,
blackened with age and smoke,
and on them were nailed and hung
iron pots and pans, earthenware jugs,
tin pails and plastic buckets,
strings of onion and garlic and chilli,
and a basket of eggs, and rusty tin cans
      of dry withered herbs.
A tan-and-cream goatskin was stretched
on a length of bamboo hung on rope
      tied to the rafters,
and a black swarm of flies flew
in a maddened frenzy about the underskin.

The short, plump figure of mamá
was almost obscured by a belch of smoke
      around her
as she hand-scooped beans into a pot,
a lively, intent look on her homely face.
"Papá's in his room, I think...."
as Julia's eyes darted over the main
      building of the homestead ;
walls of grey *adobe* bricks
and stones set in mortar ;
a roof of weathered, broken red tiles,
and a roofed porch of corrugated asbestos sheeting,
with a new overhang of freshly-scented thatch
      golden in the sunlight.

On the walls were hung, like a collage mural,
straw sombreros, and a Funghans' clock
which chimed the quarter hour in musical tones;
reed cages of doves and a parrot and plovers,
and a fragile-looking grey-and-white bird
which, much to the general amusement
    of the household,
hopped tirelessly all day long.

And there were coils of rope and rusty *machetes*
and farm implements in an advanced state of erosion,
and dilapidated leather saddles and harnesses;
narrow plywood shelves on which stood
gasoline lamps and kerosene lanterns,
tins and jars of medical ointments
to cure stings and bites and scalds;
squat packets of rifle ammunition of .22 calibre,
bobbin reels of cotton and balls of wool,
candles and bottles and old spent batteries;
small plastic bags containing a miscellaneous
jumble of gewgaws,rosary beads,
and small silver cruxifixes on finely linked chains,
and miniature portraits of the saints,
scissors and comics and penknives -
    and all these things were coated
    with a fine grey dust.

"Maybe mamá will let us go to market today...."
Against the wall on the porch
leaned crates of empty Coca-Cola bottles
and burlap sacks of corn husks;
a bale of sugar with mouse droppings in it,
water jars and a large water barrel;
gunny sacks of beans and rice and corn,
and a vintage waggon wheel
with half its spokes missing -
and the sun shone dully on these things.

"Mamá will need more vegetables eh, Ruth ?"
Jutting out beyond the porch
was a low fencing of latticed boards
        and trellised reed cane,
and it was here where mamá kept her herb garden
        in tin cans wired to the fencing.
There were small-leafed green plants
twisting and creeping through the trellis;
plants tumbling out of their tins in abundance
and cascading over other plants,
their sharp scents mingling;
yellow camomiles drinking sun rays;
pretty *chía* plants with deep blue flowers
shaped like small soup bowls;
chela plants, rosemary and mint and oregano.
And there were tiny, delicate rose-pink flowers
with emerald green cloaks of crinkled leaves;
a flaming mass of red and purple jessamines;
and a peppering of platinum-white blossoms
hiding behind thick,olive-green foliage -
and insects worked in a most businesslike manner
about these flowers and plants.

"Oooh, Christina is at it !"
A young woman, wearing a white blouse
and a long, full skirt with a print
        of stylized exotic birds,
was sweeping the hard-baked dirt yard
        with a rush broom.
She raised the broom to scatter a hen
        and its chicks,
and the hen clucked and chuckled
and bounced over the yard,
its head jerking to and fro,
and the chicks followed in quick, nervous runs,
like fluffy yellow balls blown by gusts of wind.
The rush broom stroked the ground
        lifting crisp sepia dust.

A turkeycock gobbled hysterically
fluffing its canopy of riotous coloured feathers,
moving across the yard like a richly ornate
    Venetian barge.
And the broom swept the dust,
and the dust rose up like particles of gold
in the light of the sun.

The *señorita* worked her way over to shade trees
of beech and ash and beefwood,
of guava and mesquite and tamarind,
and the dust she raised fell
as a thin mantle over dark-green shrubs and bushes
humped around the trunks of these trees.
Her ears unconciously caught
the monotonous symphony of droning insects
    in the upper branches,
and crimson-and-black butterflies flitted
above her head like scraps of paper
    teased by a wind.
She skirted around a brown-bristled hog
snorting and grunting with great indignation,
its forelegs hobbled in true country style.

There was a sudden raucous shriek
of the parrot on the porch,
and wild doves flew away in alarm
from a peach orchard beyond the yard.
And the dust swirled and eddied
in clouds about the sunny yard.

PART 7

"Ruth ! Juan's back from the fields...."

      A bareheaded boy plodded
slowly across the yard under the beating sun,
    a grey shaggy dog,
almost as big as the boy himself,
following at his heels.
The boy was bent forward slightly
under the weight of a full round basket
of fresh green fodder on his back,
held by a soft leather tumpline on his forehead.
There was a sudden flash of sun on steel,
the blade of a long, wide-curved machete
tucked bravely in the boy's belt.
He stopped at the animal pen
and swung his load to the earth,
and a silent explosion of dust
erupted around the basket.
He slid the machete from his belt
and stuck it in the ground,
and the metal whanged ringingly.
The great dog sat on its haunches
     and thumped its tail,
and hot dust spurted up,
causing the beast to sneeze.
The boy heaved the basket to his shoulder
and allowed its contents to gush
over the log fencing of the pen,
and the rich green fodder was instantly
savaged and trampled on by the animals.

The boy wiped a sheen of moisture from his forehead
with the sleeve of his sweat-dampened shirt.
He peeled off the shirt
and carelessly draped it over a post.

Then he padded silently across the yard,
and his footsteps were lighter now.
The dog followed him,
as faithful dogs that know only one master
        usually do,
its tongue out panting because of the heat,
and bushy tail waving eagerly.
The boy ambled through the wasteland patch
        of the farmhouse dump;
a ragged, untidy area of loose sandy soil
        and old ground straw,
smashed bottles and chicken feathers,
animal dung and rusty tin cans,
        and shelled corncobs.
There was a heavy, putrid smell of garbage,
attracting flies and wasps and ants.
Chicken feathers seemed alive
as they fluttered restlessly with the dust
        and a steady ground wind.
The dog trotted over the effluvium of waste,
its moist nose down and snuffing about
the heady putrescence of decay,
its overlarge ears flopping about
like two damp dish rags.

The boy was into shifting dappled sunlight
        by the shade trees.
He paused before a large clay water jar
        on the porch.
With greatly deliberate movements,
he reached for a pot mug hung on a nail
        in the porch beam
and lifted the lid off the water jar.
He dunked the mug into a dark cool well
        of water and raised it,
dripping cold silver tears,
to his dusty lips.

He remembered to sip slowly
- as he was in a sweat -
taking short breathers in between.
His eyes moved indifferently
over a grey-bodied accumulation
of junk and paraphernalia
on the homestead's central porch.
The mug was again lowered
into the shadowed depths of the water jar.
He drank his fill and rained the dregs
          over the ground,
and the dog went at once to nosy about
the dark streaks made in the dust.
For the dog's trouble it got its big wet nose
patched on the end with dust.
It shook its head and snorted like a horse.

The boy strolled casually to a rope hammock
strung between two ancient thorn trees
bleeding black sap from their trunks.
He flopped in the hammock
with a curious sigh on his lips.
The dog turned round and round
          within one spot,
as if trampling flat some grass,
as its ancestors must have done,
and the dog at last lay down
          by its master's side,
noisily panting and its salmon-pink tongue
dripping a gossamer thread of saliva.

The hammock swung in gentle arcs.
The boy could smell acrid woodsmoke
as it drifted from the kitchen,
and he heard the familiar sound
of his mamá hand-clapping *tortillas*;
and a boy who had worked in the fields
since the first light of day
waited patiently for his breakfast.

PART 8

     Doña Maria Ramos
was known as a warm and greatly affectionate woman.
    She was a true *mestizo*;
her face dark-complexioned, with laugh lines
    running from her long mouth,
    the lips full and sensual.
Lines ran in all directions like a road map
over her narrow brow and high, angular cheeks,
crinkling deeply in a 'V' formation
    from her widely-set, intensely avid eyes.
Her blue-black hair was parted in the middle,
combed back in one natural wave,
and worn in a braid tied with lilac beaded cord.
It bounced like something alive
against the small of her back
    whenever she moved.

And to those who knew her,
mamá was a strong woman,
   strong physically,
strong in mind and character,
a woman of indomitable spirit.
And one who possessed a homely sense of humour.
Mamá's every gesture and movement
bespoke careful practicality and skill,
and with an authority worthy of anyone's respect.
Her hands were swift-moving and sure;
    clever, expressive, one might say eloquent.
And there was about her at all times
a gentle tenderness and commanding dignity.
Such were the excellent qualities of mamá.

A chicken squawked and helplessly flapped
its wings, hung upside down,
its shanks firmly gripped by mamá.
The fowl feebly struggled
in her strong brown hand.

She smiled at the severe face with its gunmetal eyes,
for a reason which she could not ever explain,
had she given the matter any thought.
Perhaps it was that her subconcious mind
saw the bird as a symbol of essential food
and nourishment for her family.
With a sigh then, and a brief twinkle of resolve
        in her eyes,
mamá stunned the fowl with a snappy knuckle rap
and lowered it into a large pot
of furiously bubbling water,
and she held the bird there
until its shanks stiffened and stilled.

Moments later, plucked and singed clean,
its healthy plumpness and fresh odour
attracting a small squadron of flies,
the chicken was ready for gutting and the stockpot.
Mamá cut into it, with deft
graceful strokes of a knife,
and there was an almost devilish smile
of triumph on mamá's face.

Two cats mewed imperatively under her feet
as she hand-fanned a glut of warm-stirred flies
around a pail of smoking entrails and feathers.
One of the cats daringly jumped up
and snatched at the food with its small sharp teeth,
and pinkish purple entrails slivered
        over the rim of the pail.
Mamá wiped a streak of blood
off the chicken's breast
with a piece of gunny sacking,
and the two cats fought an earnest game
of tug-of-war with a long string of intestine.

"Away with you, *ándale* !" mamá snapped
clapping her hands,

and the cats ran off,
dragging the tube of intestine
    through the dust,
    and flies followed.

The chicken was put in a stockpot,
with an onion chopped in quarters
and half a hand of course rock salt.
That done, mamá lifted a pail of corn dough
and placed it on a stone slab by the hearth,
where stood a three-legged stone *metate*.
She rinsed down this grinding stone
and slapped half the corn dough on it.
Then she picked up a *mano*
    (or stone rolling pin)
and began to grind the corn,
her body leaning forward a bit,
her arm muscles rippling.
And the dough turned to a smooth
light grey paste under the motion of the roller.

Girlish laughter caused mamá
to look up from her work.
Julia and Ruth came skipping across the yard,
Christina not far behind them,
still sweeping dust and splintered sunlight.
The boy Juan ambled over as well,
    with the dog predictably
    close on his heels.
And mamá glanced at her brood
    with amused tenderness.
Little Julia was first to reach her,
and the child threw herself with gay abandon
into the folds of mamá's skirt of homespun wool.

"Mamá !" cried Julia, fresh-eyed
and hardly able to contain her delight.
"Is señor Ramírez coming today ?"

"Who? Oh Pancho ! Sí, I think he will,"
and mamá gazed down quietly and fondly
into her daughter's sparkling eyes.

"Good morning, mamá," Ruth smiled
and kissed her mother's hand.

Julia bounced about springily
        and joyfully cried :
"Oh señor Ramírez !
        Oh Pancho Pancho !
        Pancho Ramírez !"

"That's enough, *muchacha*," said mamá,
in a tone of mocking remonstrance.
And Julia moved on to another tack :
"We're going to pick flowers for you,"
        she burbled happily.
        "Me and Ruth."
"Flowers ? From where, might I ask ?"
"Of course, mamá !"
"Of course what ?"
"*You might ask*, of course !"
"Well where then ?" laughed mamá.
"From your garden, where else !"
"Ahh, that's nice...."

"It'll be a good market today, mamá,"
said Juan, getting in his piece.
"That's a wonder, Juanito," mamá said,
"what with having no rain for months."
"Lots of stuff, mamá, cartloads of it,"
said Juan, casting an eye on Christina,
who began to pour water into a can
        from a large bucket,
while the parrot on the porch
gave her a wolf-whistle
following that with an insane shriek.

I'll send the girls along shortly,"
mamá told Juan, who still watched Christina
flicking water over the yard
in an effort to settle the dust.
"Sí, mamá," said Juan, and sat himself down
on a wooden three-legged stool,
the dog hard by him,
vigorously scratching itself.

Juan ran a hand through
his shock of jet-black hair.
Like most other boys who lived
in the remote and isolated *rancherías*
and *pueblos* of Mexico,
Juan was mature in his manner
far beyond his young years.
His face showed an exprssion
of deep inward thought,
indicating a more than usual intelligence;
an intelligence reflected plainly
enough in his eyes,
which missed nothing and saw everything,
with a clarity and understanding
which never failed to amaze
and gratify his proud parents.

He caught mamá's gaze on him now,
and mamá could sense the emotions
thrilling through him.
She smiled, not at her son so much,
but at the fact that his head
was pefectly level with that of the dog
as it sat and looked at its master
with old and wise,
rather mournful eyes.

PART 9

"Are we having
something special for *comida*, mamá ?"
asked Julia,
unusual seriousness in the tone of voice
and in the expression on her face.
"*Enchiladas*," suggested Ruth.
"With *Mole* sauce," Julia added.
"Chicken *caldo* with mint and lemon."
"With tomatoes and onion too."
"We could have *posole*. I love posole !"
"Sí Rutí, with radishes and cabbage,
all cut up in long thin bits."
"You eat lettuce with posole."
"No Rutí, cabbage!"
"Lettuce."
"Cabbage!"
"It's lettuce, Julia."
"Ah sí, and star pasta. Mamá,
can we have star pasta for comida ?"
"Ahh *mí madre!*" exclaimed mamá laughingly.
"Pancho likes *tamales*," said Juan,
getting in his little bit again.
"That's it mamá! And I'll sort it out,"
Julia burst out all of a sudden.
"You make the tamales, Juan;
and you Rutí, help mamá with tortillas.
And Christina can pick the orange leaves
for some *ponche*,
and chop the chillies -
Chop-the-chillies!
Chop-the-chillies! (singing)
- and sift the beans and cook the stars
no, mamá can cook the stars,
she knows best how and -
sí, the lemon grass, Christina,
pick the lemon-grass,

and put the corn to soak and -"
"Is that all!" Christina almost exploded.
"We shall see what we can do," put in mamá.

She lifted a hand of brown speckled eggs
        from a basket.
The eggs were fresh and still warm
        from the laying,
and mamá felt their warmness
in the palms of her hands.
Long plumes of bluish smoke
rose from the hearth fire
and stickwood spat and crackled
in the belligerent blaze of orange flames.
Mamá fired a blackened skillet
and dexterously cracked in four eggs.

            "Sit yourselves!"
she called over her shoulder,
her face in smoke puffing from the hearth.
        "Quickly now, ándale!"

Ruth began to hum a love song
- *me abandonas* -
and Julia tried to whistle.
            "Hurry it now!"
said the imperative voice,
and mamá turned and grabbed Julia.
She tweaked her ear, to remind the child
that an order was an order,
and plonked her on a stool by the table.

"Go and find papá, Juanito,"
        mamá commanded lightly,
"and have him wash his hands
before he sits-and Juanito,
put your shirt on, *por favor*."

Mamá flipped the tortillas on the *comal*,
a spatula reaching over
to baste the spluttering eggs.
Her eyes glanced dartingly from the bean pot
to an earthenware jug of boiling milk.
The milk was rising fast
to the rim of the jug,
and mamá thrust a free hand in a pail of water
and shook drops from her fingers into the jug,
and the small crisis was over as the milk sank.
She pushed the jug away from the flames
and skimmed off the skin with a spoon,
flicked it on the ground
for the cats to fight over.

"Where's papá?" asked Julia.
"I'll cut the melon," Ruth offered,
        rising from her stool.
"Ay, Ruth," mamá called from the kitchen smoke.
She glanced at the pot of beans,
and the beans jigged about as beans do
        in rapidly boiling water.
She stirred the pot a little bit
        and the beans settled,
        simmering gently now
in their purple-black cooking liquor.

"Where has papá got to?"
Julia asked obstinately,
her small voice rising,
and tossing her head
to clear her hair.

Then papá made his appearance.

PART 10

Don Antonio
was unusually tall for a Mexican,
and, as though ashamedly
aware of the fact,
deliberately stooped his shoulders
a fraction when he walked.
He had large and round
rather staring eyes
and high, blackly-etched eyebrows,
which gave him a somewhat surprised,
almost incredulous expression
on his olive-tinted face.

"Sit yourself down, *papacíto*,"
mamá urged him warmly,
and he obediently sat on a high-backed reed chair
in his accustomed place at the head of the table.
"The girls are full of it today,"
mamá went on,
a humorous light in her eyes,
"on account of Pancho coming later on."

"Uh-uh," said don Antonio,
by his nature a man of few words,
but when he did
it was usually with religious undertones,
for don Antonio was a devout Catholic.

Ruth returned with a giant-sized
ripe watermelon,
and she expertly cut into it
with a long-bladed knife.
And at last the family seated themselves;
papá and Juan, Christina and Ruth,
and the dynamic ball of energy
that was Julia.

Mamá paused in her work for a snatch of time
      to look them over,
as a hen would with its chicks.
A platter of eggs was placed
      on the rough wooden table,
and steaming tortillas wrapped in a towel
      in a tule basket.
There was a homely clatter of dishes
as the eggs were shared out by Christina.
Don Antonio crossed himself,
and the others followed suit.

"Pancho's coming over today, papá,"
      Julia said importantly,
as she bobbed her little head
to get the hair out of her eyes
and to let the sunshine in.
"If God wills it," murmured don Antonio,
smiling faintly, "then so be it,"
then his protruberant eye rested
      on the dish before him.

"At what time will he come ?"
      asked Ruth,
and she looked across the table
at Juan for the answer.
Juan felt a choking excitement
in his chest, and he cleared his throat.
"Late afternoon, I suppose," he said.
"I'll go and meet him at the Shrine."
"That'll be nice," mamá commented.
Oh Pancho !" and Julia was about to rise.
"Sit down, you !" ordered Christina.
"And button your lip," mamá warned.

The beans in the pot on the hearth
were now cooked good and soft,

and mamá heaped a full dish of them
and put the smoking dish
   before her husband.
Steam rose to his nostrils.
   With a kitchen knife
mamá began to chop an onion,
chopped it fine in the palm
of her hand over papá's dish,
and he smelt the sharp pungency
of the onion as it rained in the dish.

Mamá turned her attention to Ruth,
and said to the girl:
"I want you to go to market, Ruth,
immediately after you've eaten.
And take Julia with you
   as I've much to do."
"Sí, mamá."
"Get some big fat tomatoes, hey mamá !"
   squeaked the little one.
"More tortillas, papacíto ?" mamá asked,
while Ruth passed wedges of watermelon
   round the table.
"Round and smooth big fat tomatoes...."
"There you are, asking for a clip."
"Eat your melon, child," papá ordered.

Julia held a huge wedge of watermelon
   in her tiny hands.
"Look, mamá," she opened up again,
"this is our flag, in this melon."
"Indeed little one, and how is that ?"
"Maestra told us at school, mamá.
See" - Julia tapped a finger
   on the dark green rind -
"here's the green, for independence,
and here is the white, that's for -
   - hmm, it means -"
"For religion," Ruth put in quick,

"For religion," Ruth put in quick,
        glancing at papá.
Julia ignored her and went on,
        her finger pushing into
the soft flesh of the fruit.
"White is for religion,
and the red part, mamá,
the red is for the union."
"The union of what ?" asked mamá.
"The union !" Julia emphasised.
"Sí, but what union ?"
"Of the races, mamá," Ruth said sweetly,
and as sweetly smiled at her sister,
who promptly pouted her lips,
        then sank her teeth
into the soft pulp of the fruit.
"And what are the little black things ?"
        asked mamá in all innocence.
"Oh mamá !" cried Julia in vexation,
        "they're the seeds !"
which coughed up a laugh from papá.

As the meal neared its end,
the family left the table in ones,
leaving just Juan and the dog.
Mamá poked the embers of the fire,
        and with a dampened rag
she swabbed the old stone slab
        by the hearth
then turned and said to Juan:
"You'd better take the hog
and deliver it to don Roberto."
"Sí, mamá," Juan said blandly,
his tongue wrangling out melon seeds.
        He spat seeds on the ground,
and the dog's nose end twitched
        and its eyes blinked.

68

"And, Juanito," mamá said, "if you see him,
        old Pancho I mean,
tell him he's to take comida with us.
as I'm sure he's forgotten, bless him.
Well, he hasn't been for some time,
and - very well, that's settled -
Off you go then son, ándale."
And in a flash Juan was up from his stool
and striding across the yard.
        The dog shot up
and its ears rose like candle flames.
It started to follow,
and then suddenly stopped,
turned its head back,
hoping against hope itself
that the woman in the kitchen
would throw it a tortilla or two.

PART 11

   Birds chittered
in the branches of a tree overhanging
the tumbledown, sun-blistered stable.
Juan looked up and saw tatters of straw
and leaden-white stains of birdlime
      under the eaves
where the birds were nesting.
He opened the stable doors
and entered the woolly gloom,
a nimbus of flies about his head.
The air in the stable pulsed
      with black swarms
      of the maddened insects,
and there was a sharp ammoniac reek
      of horse piss,
always at its strongest in the morning.

Juan's boots ploughed through
rank-smelling swathes of corn straw
and dollops of fresh manure
      to his horse
stamping skittishly in the end stall.

"Impatient today eh, my Chapulín ?"
      Juan murmured fondly,
patting the horse's croup,
and the horse whickered with pleasure,
and a spray of dust fell from the stalltop.

The horse was a handsome,
toasted chestnut-brown bay,
well-muscled and long-tailed,
with alert, sharply pointed ears.

There was an appealing expression
        in its nut-coloured eyes
as it swung its head
to nuzzle the boy's shoulder.
Why he should have named the horse
        Chapulín, meaning grasshopper,
        no one knew.
Chapulín gave the boy a
'Well, you're here at last
        and about time too!'
        sort of look,
then blinked at the sunlight
slicing through the open stable doors.

Juan led him out
of the ramshackle stable,
hooves plopping heavily on thick manure
        and urine-sodden ground straw,
to the farmstead's tilt-cart
        in the sun-drenched yard.
The cart shafts stuck in the air
        like a pair of cannon,
        dripping rusty trace chains
        and sun-hot leather harness.
Dust-devils waltzed across the yard,
and Chapulín tossed his head
        and twitched his ears
at the pestiferous insects about him.

"Easy, hombre," Juan commanded
        softly in the horse's ear.
He would need some help to hitch
        him to the tilt-cart,
        and his eyes pinned on papá,
who was quietly sitting on a wooden keg
in the shade of a nearby burro stall,
busily twining strands of rope hemp,

and obviously oblivious of the bombastic heat
and the droning hum of flies in the stall.

"Papá, could you spare a moment, por favor ?"
        Juan called to him,
and don Antonio came straight over.
He tidied up a tangled knot in the trace chains,
and the links clinked with an oddly musical sound.
"Where are you off, my son ?" he inquired,
        in his quiet sonorous voice.
"The hacienda, papá," Juan replied,
slipping the snaffle on Chapulín.

Papá lifted the shaft and they hitched
        the horse to the tilt-cart,
as scrawny chickens pecked and grubbed
at dirt dangerously close to the horse's hooves.
"You're taking the hog," asked papá,
        dropping in the last linch-pin.
"Sí, papá."
"Paid in advance, did he, Roberto ?"
"Sí, papá, as he usually does."
"And has he seen the hog ? No, he hasn't,"
don Antonio answered himself.
"A man ought always to look
over what he intends to buy.
But still, it's a sale for us,"
and papá watched Chapulín's pointed ears
        flick at the tormenting flies.

They heard a bird warbling gaily
to its mate somewhere in the orchard,
and the dog came trotting to them.
It sank to its knees in the dust
and stretched its front legs out,
chin resting in a bowl of dust.
The heat of the day raised
the dung odour from the stable,
and it drifted over to them.

The dog sniffed at the pungent scent
and closed one eye, then the other.
Juan picked fussily at loose threads
curling from the edge of the saddle-cloth,
as the homely lilting melody
 of *El siete legüas*
 floated towards him,
through the hot morning air
from the pueblo across the river.

"I'll go and get the hog," said Juan,
and he spun on his heels and strode off,
leaving papá to patiently wait
under the heavy, swelling heat.
Juan returned moments later
drubbing the hog with a stick.
The beast's underbelly was caked
 with dirt and dust,
and it smelt abominably.
It tried to turn and Juan
gave it a whack with the stick
across the middle of its
 roughly bristled back.

The man and the boy hoisted the hog
 into the tilt-cart,
and the hog kicked up a fuss,
thudding the cart bed with its hind hooves,
snorting and snuffing angrily.
Dung and dried mud fell from it,
like fragments of clay pottery.
Juan speedily tied its rope halter
 to the seat stanchion.
"There, you stink !" he snapped
and he slammed down the tail-gate.

Juan was up now on the cart
and loosely gathered the reins,

while the dog at once led off.
Juan gave a short curt command
and Chapulín began to strain at the traces,
snorting with effort and tossing his mane.
     The traces tautened,
and the cart shuddered and groaned,
the wheels creaking and rattling.

"Wait ! *Un momento* ! Just a moment!"
Mamá came waddling ponderously
along the path from the farmhouse,
          puffing and panting,
listing slightly with the weight
of a bulging string bag
tucked like a chicken under one arm,
and Juan brought the horse to a halt
and turned in his seat.

"What is it, mamá ?"
"Here, take this," said mamá flusteringly,
quite out of breath with her exertions,
"some fruit for the rancheros.
          Puff....puff....apples."
(*A fine example of the Mexican way
of doing things at the last moment* !)

Mamá patted her brow,
her mouth in an 'O' shape.
She got her breath back and said :
"They're small ones and a bit hard,
to be sure,but what can you expect
at this time of the year, hey ?"
"Put them in the back, mamá."
"What,and have the hog get them !"
"Here, then," laughed Juan,
and mamá dropped the bag between his feet.

"Off with you then," mamá ordered,
throwing out a hand
as though it held a knout. "Ándale !"
"Okay, *hasta luego*. Ay-ya, Chapulín !"
and metal jingled, old leather squeaked,
        wood creaked,
and once more they were on their way.

A cock strutted and capered boldly before them,
a hen and a posse of chicks pattering after it.
The dog turned at a fork in the track,
enveloped in a haze of dust,
and Chapulín cheerfully followed,
the cart grinding and rumbling
and looking very likely as if
it would crumble into pieces at any moment.
The tail-gate shook and the hog shivered,
squealing, and losing its footing.
The wheels scraped and jarred over hummocks,
ruts and bumps, rubble of stone and rock.
And the cart left behind
a swirling trail of gold-washed dust
        caught by the sun.

PART 12

          The forenoon heat came
over the land like the calescent
          breath of Satan,
          and Ruth and Julia,
on their way to the market in the pueblo,
were beyond a wood surrounding the farmstead,
treading a pebbled pathway along the edge
of a gently sloping cornfield near the river.

A man was ploughing the field
with a pair of large-eyed, sad-eyed oxen,
the beasts' heads yoked together
with a batten of timber.
And this oxen team was nearing the end
          of a long straight furrow.

"Ayarrh! Yarrh!" called the *milpero*,
thrusting a long steel tipped rod
into the hides of the lumbering animals
with typical Mexican indifference
                    to cruelty.

"Yarrh! Yarrh!"
And the man was forced to lift his feet high
          as he followed the team
in the loose dry sandy furrow.
"Yarrh!" he threw out mechanically
          and without thought,
as though he also were a beast of burden.

Then he soon reached the furrow end
and gratefully let go of the plough handle.
"Phew!" he breathed heavily,
muttering to himself all the while,
as lone labourers of the land
          are apt to do.

He wiped his brow
with the back of his hand
and flicked granular sweat
into the parching soil.
Then he rested a dusty boot
on a clod of earth; and,
with blunt, sunburned, calloused fingers,
he tremblingly rolled himself a *cigarro*,
and all this while quite unaware
            of the girls presence.

"That be it, Curro,"
the milpero drawled to himself,
"you've done well enough, uцy!"
and he sucked hungrily
on the thinly rolled cigarette,
muttering away between puffs.

"Come on," urged Ruth,
tugging at her sister's arm.
They hurried on, and the milpero
had not known of their passing by.
He stood gazing into the distance
with weary sun-hurt eyes.
And the hard fervid sun
            was getting higher.

Ruth and Julia arrived at the river,
or rather the dry riverbed;
but there was a slight stream
trickling slugishly and silently,
threading the bed near the opposite bank.
The girls paused at a curve of the cutbank
to watch a group of women beating
out their washing in the ridged bottoms
of wooden troughs by the stream.

Washed garments, raggéd with constant beating,
were spread like tropical blossoms
over bushes to dry in the sun.

The girls took their feet
down earthen steps roughly carved
    out of the cutbank.
One of the women turned at that moment
and smiled at them with a simple, bovine face.
A passel of thin, button-eyed children
played in green-slimed sinkholes
    stamped in the riverbed,
chuntering away among themselves
    like ground squirrels.
One shrimp of a boy, unabashedly naked,
played alone at the edge of the stream,
    skimming flat stones
    across the brief span of water
    reflecting dazzling sunlight.

Insects flew in spiraling configurations
just above the surface
of the glassy backwaters by the bank
and sounding like a faraway windstorm.
And there was a mellifluous chattering
of two young bluejays
    in the tasseled reeds.
The sun was now several hours
    above the cordillera,
a hard blasting fireball
beating mercilessly
on the backs of the women.

Julia scooted across the gravelled riverbed,
the child's vital energy not yet worn down
    by the sweltering heat.

Her flying braids flashed silver-blue
   in the incandescent sunlight.
Ruth caught up with her,
and in the clear blue sky
the sun hung hard and dazzling.

They were into scrub grass
scorched brown and dull with dust,
Julia stompingly followed an ants' trail,
   Ruth behind her
and walking in her dust.
Grasshoppers jumped on ahead
of them in the dry sapless grass;
and the 'hoppers sounded
like the snapping of small, brittle twigs.
The girls bypassed thickets
of dusty, thorny scrub in the shimmering heat,
and at length arrived
at the pueblo of San Angelo del castillo.

PART 13

       The pueblo was formed
of two quadrangles of *adobe* huts
     juxtapositioned to a *plaza*,
      and boasting gardens, dirt yards, corrals,
small orchards of lemon and avocado trees.

Ruth and Julia walked down a narrow by-lane
lined by impenetrable walls of thorny bushes
       and organ cactus.
And at last they approached the plaza itself,
a bright hot dusty square of open ground
centred by a crudely built bandstand,
swarming with noisy children of the village.
There were a few dust-spattered shade trees
and prickly pear cacti scattered here and there,
and tree trunk benches
where sat small convivial groups
of idlers supping *tequila*,
and an old and rusty water pump.
Looking onto the plaza was an ancient stone chapel,
a one-roomed federal primary school,
a *tienda* (or shop) or two, a corn mill
      and a *cantina*,
       and the open market-place.

There was a general air of gaiety about the plaza,
especially in the vicinity of the market,
that recognised social meeting ground
      of the Mexican peasantry.
Waves of sunburnt, black-eyed people
chivvied and bunted among the sunsplashed stalls.
They gesticulated expressively
and conversed in soft, subdued, musical tones,
exchanging sincere pleasantries
with timeworn simplicity and naturalness.

They crowded around the booths
which were festooned with coloured streamers
        and flower garlands;
they promenaded the dust-spumed square walk
        of the plaza;
and the very dust in the air
had a fragrance of its own,
spiced with cinnamon and burned chillies.

The people bartered quietly but persuasively,
joking and spitting and laughing
        softly with their eyes.
A man was playing a guitar
on the stone step of the cantina,
and bands of unwashed children
came running out of the yards and side alleys
to join the hubbub in the plaza,
and dogs chased after them.
The air trembled festively,
for the phonograph music
was unmistakably at its loudest here.

Here then was the real land of *México*.
This was the true gritty essence
of the country and of its people.
It was all evident here
in the primordial smell
of horses tethered by the cantina;
a drove of goats dipping their beards
to the dust of the ground
as they clipped across the plaza;
hobbled pigs rolling
in their own filth
in the shade of clapboard
        and canvas booths.

Under this blazing Mexican sun
were the people, poor peasantry ! *Indeed* !
    Buying and selling,
        buying and selling,
trading their homemade wares;
        straw-woven baskets,
        grain and fruit,
        raw goatskins,
and primitively moulded,
        thickly glazed pottery,
bright with brazen colours,
against the sunstream light.
Smiling mostly, these country folk,
jostling and gently pushing,
smiling and sociably murmuring
        to one another:
"*Con permiso*, with your permission...."
said a jolly broad-cheeked stout woman
carrying baskets upon baskets
        of flowers in her arms
        and on her head.
"Sí, yes, *pasale*," replied a little woman,
        rather short-sighted,
nosing into the heady bouquet
and at the same time trying
to get out of the other's way.
"*Oye,* don Carlos!" called a smart ranchero
with thick moustache covering
the lower half of a merry, good-natured face.
        "Buenos días!"
"Buenos días! *Que paso, amigo* ?"
        said his friend,
equally smartish in buckskin shirt,
        striped ranchero pantaloons
tucked in Léon leather knee-length boots,
and the two of them put heads together
        chatting for all their worth.
"Oh, *muy bien* -very good!" said someone.
"*Perdonomé* -excuse me," said another.

"*Gracias, señor.*"
   "Esperanza! *Hola!*"
   "Ah, doña Margarita,
you'll never guess what I heard...."
   "*Oye, compadre!*"
   "Why, it's Frontino himself!"
   "Con permiso...."
   "Pasale, señora...."
   "Gracias, gracias...."
And so it went on all over the market.

A couple of drunken *mestizos* crashed out
through the double swing-doors
      of the cantina.
They lurched and canted across
      the inflamed plaza,
hanging onto each other for support.
Then one of them stopped,
a thickset man of forty,
and tried to adjust the buckle of his belt
      lost under a swollen paunch.
The other man, filthy and derelict,
      suddenly vomited,
and it spurted out as though
      expelled by a pump,
and splattered over the hard dusty ground
      with a soft slap.
A mongrel trotted up on rickety legs
and sniffed with hope and greedy eyes.
Another dog appeared, then another.
The dogs snuffled and gobbled
the thick splay of vomit,
incuriously watched by hard-faced rancheros
dressed in dusty rawhide and denim.
The dogs ran off, and the ground
was hammered dry again by a pace
      of pack-burros.

PART 14

      Ruth and Julia
sauntered happily between the stalls
displaying piles of tomatoes, onions and chillies,
papayas and yellow mangoes and purple-hued guavas.
At one stall three pretty señoritas
with dark flashing eyes and laughing faces
were cooking corncakes over braziers
in astonishingly prodigious amounts.
At another stall hard by,
melon and squash seeds were roasting on griddles,
giving off a tantalising sweet nutty odour.

Ruth stopped for a moment at a booth
selling brightly coloured bolts of cotton print,
and she was unable to resist spading a hand
under a length of material
which had instantly caught her eye;
plum-coloured cotton with slashes
of powder blue and aquamarine.
And they moved on between the tiny stalls,
carefully jostled by the milling crowds.

      A bird warbled
beyond the chapel's sun-dipped bell-tower,
and there was an unceasing crowing
      of cocks in the yards,
and dogs sniffing the ground
      of the plaza
mellow with fruity fragrances
coming from the stalls.
A muleteer entered the dusty square
      from the east side,
leading a drove of mules laden with stickwood
golden brown
under the brightness of the sun.

The mule at the rear
of the short caravan stopped itself.
It blew heavily and noisily
    in the hot dusty air,
then angled its knobbled hindlegs
in the unmistakable stance
of an animal about to shit,
and it did indeed do so,
its agate eyes fixed on
an illimitable point in space.
That done, the mule twitched
its ears and clopped on,
with a somewhat easier gait,
and Julia followed behind it,
stepping over a smouldering
    monk-brown heap of dung.

Ruth's attention was taken by a little girl,
    skinny and bedraggled,
who was chewing on a stick of sugar cane.
The child wore one oversized shoe
and she hobbled and gimped
slantwise down the street;
and it was that peculiar walk
which reminded Ruth of señor Ramírez,
    better known as Pancho,
who walked like that naturally.
The child paused a second at a corner
in order to gain equilibrium,
though tilting like a keeling skittle,
    then disappeared from view.

The girls were now at a fruit and vegetable booth,
and behind pyramids of tomatoes sat an old woman
Her face dark and creased as a prune.

She smiled at them, all wrinkles,
her teeth small and stained,
like unhusked grains of rice.

"Fresh picked, as new flowers.
Like you, my little blossoms,"
she said in warm, full round tones,
indicating the fruit with flapping hands.

Ruth's cheeks flushed with pleasure,
while Julia simply looked at the woman,
all innocent-eyed and respectfully angelic.
"How much for one kilo ?" Ruth asked,
pointing to the tomatoes.
The old woman seemed to deliberate,
then replied: "Eight *pesos*, my flower,
          is that all right for you ?"
and she fondled a tomato
perched on the top of a pyramid stack.

Ruth did not say anything immediately,
but permitted herself a smile
with that elemental naïvete of the young.
There was no doubt at all in the woman's mind
that this girl would purchase something
          or other from her,
and her irrefragable conviction
did not prevent her from pursuing
the exercise of bantering sales talk,
as much a necessity of social discourse
than the rather materialistic effort
of selling fruit itself.
And so the old woman and Ruth
          and even little Julia
all three wagged in spunky ebullience,
in that extraordinary way
commonly found in simple, age-old cultures.

"Seven-fifty, señora ?"
"Oh, I couldn't possibly."
"They're beautiful."
"Sí, aren't they ?"
"It's a hot busy day "
"To be sure, my angel."
"Well, let me think now."
"Take your time, my lovely."
"Can I just feel one ?"
"Oh sí, help yourself,"
and the woman's hands flapped
    with elaborate gestures.
"Seven seventy-five," Julia spoke up,
going the wrong way.
Ruth pulled a face at her.
"Ah, you're such a pretty one,"
the old woman said in her warm rolling tones.
"Both of you. So let's say seven pesos, hm ?"
"Six pesos, fifty *centavos*," Ruth compromised,
and the old woman laughed,
sweetly and roundly like a young girl,
winking grandly. "Six pesos seventy-five."
"*Muy bien*, very good,"
Ruth agreed at once,
"two kilos, por favor."

A slant of sunlight fell
through a hole in the canvas awning of the booth
and Ruth shaded her eyes with one hand
as she watched the woman weigh
the tomatoes on old-fashioned scales.
Ruth leaned forward and could smell
the woman's breath of milky nuttiness,
as if she had been chewing toasted pumpkin seeds.

"There, my flower," the woman declared,
dropping the tomatoes into Ruth's open bag
and throwing in a small hand
of chillies as well for luck,
as they do at country markets.

The girls politely smiled,
    thanked the old woman,
    and left the booth,
into the light and heat of the sun
    and the dust of the day,
deciding to visit next
    the tienda on the plaza.
A dust-devil as tall as a horse
    galloped over the square
        in front of them.

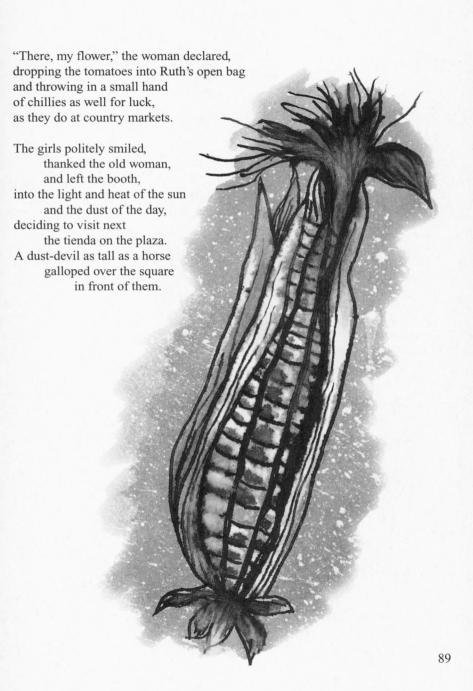

PART 15

       The short square figure of Pancho
moved around in the gloom of the stables
of his friend don Roberto's hacienda.
He was pottering about and checking the horses,
and he went from horse to horse
     with a swaying erratic gait,
like a storm-tossed boat,
as if his heavy chunkiness was too much
     for his stunted bandy legs.
His long arms hung loosely at his sides,
     fists slackly curled;
and, as his great torso listed to one side
with a drop of one shoulder
     and a rise of the other,
his arms swung in a lazy arc
     and slapped his thighs.
In this manner of movement
     Pancho pottered about,
and as he did so he talked all the while
     to the stablehand Julian.

       "And there we were,"
he was chummily saying to Julian,
not looking at him but throwing it over
his shoulder in that rough gritty tone,
"and there we were in the dead of night
and caught in a sudden downpour of rain,
looking out for that wily coyote, *uuy*.
And bless me if Manuel isn't sitting
     in the bushes all by himself, hmm.
Well, three torchlights zeroed on him
squatting there with his pants
     around his boots, *chingada*!

'Where's that animal, Manuel ?'
         we says to him.
'Where did it get to ?'
'Over that way it must be,' Manuel says,
pointing as far away as he could.
'Are you sure ?' we says,
lamps steady on him, mm.
'Why of course I'm sure,' Manuel says,
a square piece of paper in his hand,
'I saw him, didn't I? As you see me,'
he says, which gave us a good laugh
at poor Manuel's expense.
Pass the saddlecloth, Julian....
What, it's not there ?
Hmm, I wonder where I left it then ?
Where did I leave the damn thing ?
Aay, come to think on it,
I must have left it by the roan gelding's.
Carajo Pancho! Are you getting so old now
that you can't remember where
you've left things ? Come on, Julian."

Pancho rambled on amiably,
and the stablehand Julian,
who was somewhat of a simpleton,
followed Pancho like a faithful dog.

Bronze blades of light cut through
the chinks in the stable walls,
shining sharply on the flanks
of a young mare.
              Pancho paused,
running his eyes over the horse.
He hunkered down on his haunches
to inspect a mark on the mare's left fetlock,
and as he did so his face hit a cobweb
              and he softly cursed.

92

"See that, hombre ?" he growled.
"She must have done that herself,
rubbed herself with her own hoof.
It looks like a wasp's sting, eh ?"
he remarked, with something like
the assured authority of a Xenophon.
"It'll be best to rub in some of that
            -What's its name? -
that special ointment of mine, hmm,
but after she's been watered, Julian,"
            and Julian nodded,
more as an acknowledgement
        of having heard Pancho
            than one of agreement.

                        "Well."
Pancho was into his tale again,
"one of the lads, he says:
'I think I smell a skunk hereabouts.'
'No-o,' says another, 'you're mistaken,
            it's Manuel you can smell.'
Por la Madre Santisma !
Did you hear that, hombre ?
It's Manuel you can smell !'"
and a great belly roar fell from Pancho
and he raised his arm blindly
        to pat Julian on the shoulder
and he clouted a stable post instead.

Pancho stood up and scratched his armpit,
screwing his eyes and nose
        and sniffing like a dog.
It was stiflingly hot in the stables.
The ground straw stank of horse piss,
and droves of frenetic flies
seemingly owned the air.

Sweat popped on Pancho's brow,
beads of it hung on his eyebrows,
runnels of it on the weathered
seams of his face.
He crashed his way through ricks
of corn straw and sunworn saddlery
to get to a docktailed sorrel
which had foaled
just the day before.
His stumbling progress was checked
by a familiar sound
from beyond the paddock.

"Rider coming in,"
he grated succinctly. "Must be José, eh ?"

PART 16

Pancho made for the stable doors,
threshing through stooks of cornstalks,
Julian right behind him and banging
against a broken hand plough,
but following Pancho like his shadow.
The brilliant light of the forenoon sun
smacked them in the eyes
when they stepped out into the wide paddock.

The ranchero by the name of José,
on a dappled grey colt,
rode into the sunflooded yard at a good clip.
He reined in before Pancho and Julian,
swung from the saddle in one easy movement,
letting go the reins of the bridle
for Julian to grab.

"Hola !" he greeted them with a grin
showing tobacco-stained teeth.
He swept his sombrero off his head
and with a red bandanna
swabbed the sweat pouring from his face.
"Hot one, Corncob," he said,
addressing Pancho by his old nickname.

"Sí sí. Que pasó ?" Pancho asked at once.
"Did you ride over to the ridge
to check the cattle ?"
and José nodded,
slapping dust from his leather chaps.
Then he released bit and snaffle
from the foam flecked colt.
And Julian had managed to tear himself
away from Pancho in order to remove
saddle and cloth from the sweating horse.

Julian unfastened the saddle girths,
at the same time whispering
'sweet nothings' in the horse's ear.

Pancho set critical eyes
on the colt's sweaty flanks.
Splotches of yellowish foam
dropped from its mouth
and between its groin.
Clearly all this was not much to his liking,
and he hawked and spat in the dust at his feet.
"You shouldn't have ridden him
so hard in this heat,"
he mildly reprimanded the ranchero,
"there's no future in it, hombre.
Why ride a horse like that?
Uuy, what's your hurry, hmm?"

He then turned to Julian
and abruptly changed his tone;
"Que bien, Julian, walk him up and down,
but over in the shade
at the back of the stable,"
        he advised the slow-wit.
"Walk him till that ticker of his
slows down and the sweat dries on him.
Then give him a carrot for his trouble
and feed him some corn,
but not too much - do you hear? -
or we'll have him sweating all over again,"
        and so Julian turned about
        and walked the colt on.

"Well José, and don Roberto, where is he?"
Pancho's sandpapery raspiness
directed back at the ranchero,
a glitter of anger remaining in his eyes
at the way the horse had been treated.

José wiped travel sweat and dust
away with a sweep of his arm.
His fast ride-in had caused yard
and chaff dust to rise in the air
and it hung motionless in a dry heat haze.
"The boss, he rode north with the cowhands
to the *barranca*," he told Pancho
with a sheepish look on his swarthy face.
"The fencing's down most of the way
along the boundary line.
That damned whirlwind of yesterday."

"Whirlwinds do things like that."
"Sí, you're right there, Pancho,"
          said José,
reverting now to the diminutive
          of Francisco.

"And the herd ?"
"I think we lost a few head."
"Dead are they ?"
"No Pancho, just lost."
"Don Roberto out there sweating
with the rancheros, eh? Caracoles!
    That's a fine thing, is that !"
and Pancho's natural humour
      immediately returned.

"I saw a dust cloud back there
      from the pueblo way,"
said José, pushing back his sombrero
and scratching at his scalp.

"You can see it now, look,
      and coming this way."

"The Ramos waggon," Pancho guessed,
his keen eyes clapped on the distant object
distorted by heat haze and dust.
"It's the Ramos Waggon," he repeated,
"and young Juanito driving...."

PART 17

      Pancho stood like a rock
and waited for the tilt-cart to roll on in.
And soon enough Juan came into view
as he entered the dusty hacienda paddock
      on the rumbling cart.
Chapulín at once put on a show
and trotted majestically with his knees
      almost up to his jaw,
his snaffle jingling like tiny silver bells.
And not to be outdone, the dog clipped
in the lead with equally royal grace.
While the hog in the back of the cart
grunted and squealed furiously.
Juan pulled on the reins and gaily waved.
"Señor Ramirez ! Buenos días !"

"My little *compañero*, buenos días !
How goes it with you ?" Pancho roared
with his aggressive-like cheerfulness.
He doffed his sombrero in a salute
and gazed at the boy with a wide grin,
then scratched his backside and twisted
his nose both at the same time.

Juan jumped down from the cart into the dust,
and José voluntarily took control of Chapulín
      and began to unharness him.
Pancho shook the boy's hand,
a gentle clasp in the customary manner
      of the campesino,
then embraced him with his massive arms.
The dog went bounding off across the paddock
      to explore the new terrain.

A sudden dust-devil stormed frenziedly
    across the yard
and the dog went chasing after it,
and was quite mystified when
it just as suddenly vanished.

Within moments José had Chapulín unharnessed.
The cart teetered and fell back on its shaft ends,
and the hog was sent flying
and the apples burst out from the bag,
rolled round the hog's back
and stopped at the tail gate,
like balls in a slot machine.

"I've brought the hog for don Roberto,"
Juan told the old ranchero,
hooking his boot heel
on the wheel hub of the cart.
"So I see, Juanito, and there it is.
A hog for don Roberto
and the two go well together, hmm,"
and Pancho grinned at the boy
        like a wedge of orange.
Then he threw José a meaningful glance
and called over with casual affability:
"Walk him and rub him down, amigo,
before you water and feed him,"
and José went on, shrugging his shoulders.

"What shall I do with the hog ?" asked Juan.
"If I had my own way," replied Pancho,
his mirthful blue eyes resting on the boy,
"I'd bleed and gut it
and get a good roasting fire going.
Caramba ! it's a month or more
since I last teethed into pork."

100

"*Gracias*, señor - Pancho...." Juan said shyly,
"you've reminded me to tell you,
mamá says for you to take comida."
"Comida eh? Well, que bueno !
And, *ay caray*! you've reminded me too
    of something I must do,
and I almost forgot it, sinner I am.
I have to skin and gut a goat for him,
for don Roberto. But you did remind me
and the job's as good as done already,
but for all of that I've yet to skin
    and gut the damn thing.
Are you going to help me with it, hmm ?"
"Sí, I can help," said Juan.
"Que bueno, my compañero, que bueno.
Well, let's see to your Chapulín first.
Eh? Hmm, get him watered and fed
and curried and rested up for a bit.
It's a long haul from the farm
with a waggon, a boy, and a hog,"
and Pancho stumped off toward the stable
with jerking shoulders and swinging arms.

"What about the hog ?" Juan asked again.
"Leave it there for now, Juanito.
Maybe it'll roast itself in its skin
and save don Roberto's cook the trouble
    of lighting her stove.
Now compañero, let's get from under
    this damned burning sun,"
for the sun was well up
and the exposed paddock shivered
under a torrid blast of sun-blaze.

PART 18

They entered the shade
of the stables and Pancho's eyes turned
slate-blue in the semi-gloom.
Juan was pleased to see that Chapulín
had his head deep in a crib,
happily chomping away at corn straw
with his deep-cream teeth.
José stood nearby,
a curry comb locked in his fist,
watching the horse eat.

"Comida with you, eh?
That should make the day,"
Pancho went on urbanely.
"You know Juanito, I was always hungry
when I was about your age.
One time the *policia* were chasing me
down a street of a small town
up north where I lived."

"The policia were after you ?
What for ?"

"Well, the fact of the matter was,
I'd smashed the window of a house
belonging to the widow of a famous
bullfighter - I forget his name -
and she, the widow, uuy!
she was mad as hell at me."

"What happened to you ?"

Well now, I ran like a windstorm
down that street -

and my belly was groaning with hunger -
and at the bottom of the street
near the marketplace I saw old don Fuente,
who was also after me for stealing
biscuits from his tienda.
Hmm, they were in a barrel, you see,
those nice scrunchy biscuits,
and it stands to reason that if your eyes
are level with a barrelful of biscuits
- well, I did the only best thing
and snatched me a few.
And so don Fuente and the policia
        were after my tail.
I nipped through a little alley
into the market
and stopped at a fruit stall.
Coming at me from one side were the policia,
panting with their heavy carbines,
and coming at me from the other
was old Fuente, face all red and angry, uuy !"

"So what did you do ?"

"What could I do ?"
grinned Pancho villianously,
"Que va, hombre, I was hungry,
I ate the fruit from the stall !"

Then Julian tramped in,
tripping over a rush broom.
"Aha Julian, and where're you off to?
Go and get the goat from the pen, por favor."
"The goat, señor ?"
"The goat, you burro, for the don's dinner.
And tie it to the block,
while I put an edge to my skinning knife."

"Ah, the goat...."
"And as you're heading that way,
take the hog with you,"
as Pancho looked around him
in search of the grinding stone,
        his nose twitching,
as if he were about to smell it out.
He found the stone all ready for use
clamped on the side of a carpenter's bench.
He slipped his knife from its sheaf
and with the pad of his thumb
        felt its dull edge.
Then he set to with the task,
Juan winding the handle for him.
The wheel whirred and groaned
and sparks shot from it;
and flies whined too,
huge horseflies in a band of light
where the sun cut into the stables.

"Did you know, señor Ramírez -Pancho -
that Carmelita in the pueblo
is going to have a baby ?" said Juan,
his arm yanking the grinding stone handle.
"Is she now ?" said Pancho,
"and who's the father I'd like to know,"
as he tested the cutting edge
of his knife with his thumb.
"No one knows who the father is, uuy !"

Juan continued winding the handle,
not wanting to break off now
that he had fallen into a steady rhythm.
Then Pancho again put blade to stone,
and Juan watched the sparks flying
from the stone and scattering
over the straw at their feet.

"They say it might be don Cesar,"
Juan said in a whispering tone.
"Don Cesar is the father. I remember -"
"Why are you turning that handle, amigo ?"
    asked Pancho with a grin.
"Oh, are you done ?"
and Juan stopped at once,
feeling rather foolish.
"Well, a few more turns then,"
and Pancho leaned over the stone,
and Juan resumed cranking the handle,
sparks flying and the stone whining.

"I remember mamá saying
that it could be don Cesar,"
    Juan continued,
back to the thread of his thoughts,
his winding arm finding its
        rhythm once more,
"but I thought so myself, a long time back."

Pancho lowered his head to one side
    and spat, then said:
"You could be right, my compañero,
    and your mamá too, of course,"
and Pancho leaned closer to Juan
    and the whetting stone,
the brims of their sombreros touching.
Juan could smell the other's breath
and it reminded him of warm goat's milk.
"But we will know soon enough
as soon as the baby's born I guess,"
and Pancho wiped the grinding dust
off the knife blade
with two fingers and sheafed it.
Juan dropped his aching arm
and it dangled loosely at his side.

Pancho turned and made for the stable door.
"You've got the little fellow, eh ?"
he grated, listing and swinging
on his bandy legs towards Julian.
The goat, bleating itself hoarse,
was tied to the woodchopping block,
a thick tree stump in the paddock,
        charred by the sun,
hacked and scarred by axe and machete.
Pancho spat into his palms,
rubbed them together briskly,
and glanced sidelong at Juan
with a humorous glitter in his eyes.
"Let's get started then," he said.
"Julian, go and fetch the pump
and the buckets, por favor,"
and Julian hurried off again.

Pancho had in the meantime grabbed
the goat by its hindlegs and twisted
the animal to the ground.
He knelt before the animal,
        admiring its size.
And Julian returned carrying two metal
buckets and an ordinary bicycle pump.
He planted himself in what he assumed
his appointed place directly behind Pancho.
"No, round here, Julian,"
Pancho chipped him above the high
bleating of the goat.
"Come round here, hombre,
and grab them forelegs -
Juan, you hold him here, por favor,"
and Pancho let go of the forelegs.

He held the goat by its jaw over the stump
and put the smaller of the buckets under it.

He unsheafed the knife, blade glinting,
and swiftly slashed the goat's throat,
cutting through its pulsing jugular vein.
The animal's tongue slipped out
at the side of its mouth
and its eyes rolled
showing waxy white.

"It's still crying," said Juan.
"Sí, they never can shut up,
even with a cut throat,"
Pancho returned with a savage grin,
and then his face became all at once
quite serious as the animal's lifeblood
spurted out; rich, thick and crimson,
        into the bucket.
The blood gushed and splashed
and filled half the bucket.
It dripped thickly now like hot jam
from the gash in the neck
and the goat shrank in size.

"The pump. Julian, újule hombre!
where's the pump I asked you for ?"

PART 19

       Julian got the bicycle pump
and passed it quickly to Pancho,
who then pushed the nozzle end
a little way up the goat's anus.
Juan looked on in silent amusement
as Pancho pumped away with the air plunger.
"Fatten him up again, you see, hmm,
so we can skin him better,"
Pancho explained with a deadpan face.

The goat swelled like a balloon,
and Pancho pushed the point
of his knife into the throat and cut
all the way down to the testicles,
a sound not unlike that of a zipper
      being unfastened.
He then incised along all four legs
      to the fetlock joint,
and Juan, with his own knife,
began cutting away the hide
closed around the skull.
And Julian simply stood
with his knife in his hand
as though the goat
were about to run off.

The dog came and poked his snout
      in the bucket of blood.
"Hey you !" and Juan cracked him
      one on the haunch.

"This shouldn't take long, eh ?"
Pancho said with a genial grin,
giving Juan a gentle dig
in the ribs with his elbow.

But it was taking longer
than Pancho expected.

Juan took note of a large mesquite
tree nearby, with a broken lower branch,
and suggested the animal be hung there
to ease and speed the operation.
Pancho agreed, smiling proudly at the boy,
and Julian again sloped off to find some rope,
and they soon had the goat hanging by its neck
from the tree branch.

Pancho began stripping the hide
with the point of his knife,
while Julian took over to pull and knuckle,
almost tearing at the skin.
There was a mist of tiny gnats
around the goat's white gleaming skull
where its eyes boggled grotesquely
its tongue protruding stiffly
between its teeth.

" I think we're getting there,"
said Pancho with a beam
and breathing heavily through his nose.
Sweat cut channels in the dust
on his face, and there were dark stains
spreading from his armpits.
Juan stood back to watch,
and ready to be entertained
by the bubbles of bantering
sure to spill from Pancho,
and he was not disappointed !

"Ease up there a bit, hombre," Pancho started up.
"With your permission," said Julian,
"I'm doing well enough."
"Sí, you are at that,"
Pancho badgered him,
"you're like a man just married
and can't get it off fast enough."
"It's a big one," said Julian.
"What does he want with all this?
There's only him and his old maid,
for we won't get any for sure."
"The don is a pig when it comes
to meat," Pancho said.
"A goat today and a hog tomorrow,
and it lets us know he can afford it."
"Look at its belly."
"Uuy, you'd think he was a she
and in the family way."
"It was the pump that did it,"
Julian replied wittily,
flashing a smile at Juan.
"The air is still in there, is it?
That's its guts, you burro !"
"Whew! but it stinks, señor."
"Aha, and I thought it was you !"
And Pancho's breath came in dry,
sharp gasps as he fisted
at the join of hide to flesh.
He paused a moment to wipe his hand
against the bark of the tree,
then he wiped the sweat
        dripping from his brow.

And the chatter between them went on:
"Just look at the coat on him !" said Julian.
"It's more than what I've got," said Pancho.

"Well he's losing his," quipped Julian.
"Which is what happened to me,
I lost mine - why don't you pull
more to the side there, hombre ?"
"That's what I'm doing, señor."
"Just as I thought. Pull *down*, you *taco!*"
"Hey, where's its tail?"
"Between its legs, I shouldn't wonder."
"Or up its arse, he! he!"
"Listen to this one, Juan -
Are you pulling down, hombre,
or what are you doing?"
"Sí, I'm pulling down as you said."
"It doesn't seem like it.
Damned thing must be glued on."
"Oho! I've just remembered something."
"It's the first time, Julian."
"And I almost forgot...."
There was a brief silence.
"Well go on, hombre," said Pancho,
"tell us what you nearly forgot."
I've forgotten what it was now."
"Újule, you beat them all!" laughed Pancho.
"I've remembered. My grandfather's birthday."
"I didn't know you had one."
"It's his birthday tomorrow, ninety-seven."
"He's as old as that, caracoles !
I'd like to meet and talk with him."
"Oho, you can't do that, señor.
He's been dead and buried twenty-five years."
"Ho! ho! HO!" roared Pancho high-heartedly.
"Qué bueno hombre! Ho! ho! -
Did you hear that one, Juan ?"
and Pancho slapped his leg
and Juan grinned, showing all his teeth

"Here we go!" said Pancho presently.

"It's coming now, here we go !"
and with one last pulling rip
the hide was off.
Julian hung it tenderly
on the end of the branch
as if it were his best sheepskin jacket.

"Well, that broke the back of it,
though it's only skinned.
Juanito, give an eye
to where the bucket stands,"
Pancho warned, and instantly split
the belly from top to bottom
with a slashing sweep of the knife.
Balloonlike purplish-blue intestines
        spewed out,
warm and steaming and odoriferous,
sliding as a whole piece
        into the bucket.
There was a faint squeak
as the bulbous mass separated
from the rib cage and rolled out
to fill the bucket to overflowing.
Pancho lopped off the green bulb
that was the bile duct
and threw it to the dog.
"A bitter lemon for you,
perro," he grated.

Wraiths of flies appeared
as if from nowhere and settled
like soot on the innards in the bucket.
Splashes of blood in the dust
turned black with exposure to the air,
and flies gathered there as well.
"All right Julian, we'll cut him down
and you can take him to the kitchen."

"Do you want an apple, Pancho ?"
Juan asked a little while later,
remembering the bag of fruit
he had left in the tilt-cart,
and Pancho's merry blue eyes
turned on the boy as he replied:
"A big one for me, amigo,
if you please, eh?"
and he led the way to the cart.

They were presently hunkered
on their heels by the cart,
scrunching into their apples
and disinterestedly watching Julian
shambling across the sunblasted yard
with a bucket of congealed blood
in one hand and a bucket of entrails
          in the other,
and the goat strung over his back.

And it seemed to Pancho -
who always had a sense of humour -
it seemed to him as if the goat
had just taken a flying leap
          to mount Julian....!

Book Two

"Noon"

PART 1

"Doña María !"
The high piercing child's voice
split the air of the Ramos farmstead,
and mamá immediately dropped
what she had been doing
under the smoky kitchen lean-to
and came rushing out into the brilliant light
and oppressive heat of the high noon sun,
hastily wiping hands on her apron.
"Doña María-a-a !"

"*Chihuahua*! What is it, Angel ?"
she asked of a dimple-faced boy
who suddenly appeared in front of her,
panting like a puppy,
face glistening with perspiration,
streams of it filling his dimples.
"Doña Maria, you must come quickly !"
he breathlessly gasped,
"Carmelita is about to have her baby
and you better come quickly."

Mamá sighed with relief.
She was the *partera* - or midwife -
for the pueblo and knew
that it was the girl's first child.
No doubt she was panicking
before her time, mamá thought,
as young mothers are apt to do,
but all the same it was best
    to make certain.

"Are the contractions regular ?"
mamá asked with interest.

"Con-contraptions?"
and Angel's deep dimples shot
from one part of each cheek to the other.

"*Mi madre* !" mamá cried,
slapping a hand to her forehead,
"they send me a mere *muchacho*
who knows nothing of these things !"

"Pepe should have come," said Angel,
"but I was sent instead. Anyway,
Carmelita's having a baby.
Might be a litter of them,
going by her size -"
"Pssht! that's enough, muchacho."
"Señora Pozas says for don Antonio
    to come too."
Señora Pozas was the pregnant girl's mother.
"Ah, of course he must.
Well you know where he is,
go on, andalé !"
and Angel sprinted off
to don Antonio's sanctuary.

The request for don Antonio to attend
the event was natural enough,
as he was the local *rezandero*
- or layman preacher -
to give services for the dying
or for difficult deliveries.

"Angel !" mamá called from the kitchen,
swiftly setting things in order
        on the hearth. "Angel,
run back now and say we're on our way,"
and there then followed a feverish spate
of activity which instantly dispelled
the normal quietude of the noon hour.

Angel shot off like a jackrabbit,
mamá arranged and rearranged
black earthenware pots on the fire,
at the same time attempting to wrap
her rebozo about her.
Don Antonio stood like a post,
        twiddling his thumbs,
not knowing what to do or say,
simply standing there and waiting
for some measure of order
to emerge from the momentary chaos.

"Christina! Ruth !"
The parrot on the porch screamed
and clawed at the bars of its cage,
don Antonio turned and scowled at it,
and Christina came running
        from one of the rooms.

"You see to the pots here, Christina.
We have to go to the pueblo, me and papá."
"Why is that, mamá ?"
"Carmelita, it's her time, I think."
"Oh Carmelita...."
"Now where is Julia and Ruth ?"
"Are we ready ?" don Antonio inquired
politely in the background.
"Where in heaven is - Papacito,
you don't have your prayer book."
"I'll get it, papá," said Ruth,
suddenly appearing from nowhere.
"Ah Ruth, there you are, muchacha.
The chicken, Ruth, it'll soon be ready."
"Sí mamá, I know."
"Put it where the cats
won't get at it, all right ?
And find Julia to shell the corn.

That should keep her out of mischief
    while we're away."
"Shall we take a candle ?"
"Merciful heavens, papacito !
the girl's not on her deathbed,
she's going to have a baby.
Now, I'll need this soap,
and some towels and the rest of it,"
mamá said, talking to herself now
as she plunged hands deep
into a box of clean linen.

And at that point the tilt-cart
rumbled into the yard.

"Juan's back, *támbien*," said mamá
    with evident satisfaction,
stuffing towels into a string bag.
"He can take charge here.
Julia-a ! Where is the little one ?"
"She's asleep I think,"
don Antonio murmured.
"She's only been up two hours -
Juanito ! Juanito, we're off,
me and your papá to the pueblo.
Carmelita's time has come,"
as mamá soaked a hand-towel in cold water
and dropped it in a plastic bag.

"I'll take you, then," Juan offered,
leaping from the cart.
The parrot squawked and the dog barked at it.
"No, son, Chapulín will be tired.
We can walk, won't take us such a while."

"Would you shut him up," said don Antonio,
referring to the barking dog.

"It's the parrot, papá."
"It's the dog," said don Antonio,
"please quieten him."
"Go and find Julia," mamá said,
"and set her on the corn.
Christina will take care of the fire.
And Ruth, don't forget the chicken.
Juanito, your Chapulín looks dry,
must be he needs a drink, you think?
Well come on, papacito,
I have to deliver a child this day,
not celebrate its birthday,"
and mamá waddled off
with purposeful strides,
the speed of which
amazed them all.

PART 2

"You go on, María,
and I'll be with you later," don Antonio
told his worthy wife at the door
of the chapel in the pueblo.
"I'll pray to the saints for an easy birth,"
and he entered the stone chapel,
his sombrero in his hands,
fingers toying with the narrow
leather band of the crown.

It was still and quiet and peaceful
        in the chapel,
and there was a smell of mustiness
and stale incense in the cool air.
Outside sounds were muffled,
unable to seep through
the thick stone walls.
Dappled scallops of golden light
played on the dark slate floor,
winging in from a dusty cupola above.

Don Antonio crossed himself and moved
silently toward the humble side altar
which was devoted to the saints.
He lit two candles of rich yellow beeswax
and burned incense of lavender and rosemary.
He signed the cross toward the alabaster
figure of his saint, San Antonio,
then knelt down on his knees,
and prayed for a time.

        Mamá had in the meantime
reached the far side of the pueblo,
        freely perspiring
under the broiling noonday sun.

She arrived at the simple hut of the Pozas family,
a small crowd milling curiously but quietly
at the cane door of the hut,
shuffling their feet in the dust.
They moved aside deferentially to allow
a passageway for doña María,
the men removing their sombreros
    as a mark of respect.

"Go right in, por favor, doña María,"
said a voice, and mamá recognised señor Pozas,
who was not working in the fields on this day
and would not be for the next three days,
as it was considered unlucky for the coming child.
And mamá nodded her head with a faint air
of dignity and without saying a word,
as she stepped into the hut,
and at once took charge of the situation.

The girl Carmelita, a pretty creature
of delicate build and wide slanting eyes,
lay sweating on a petate
on the hardtrodden dirt floor,
her mother squatting by her side
and repeatedly patting the girl's hand.
The one-room hut was low-pitched
and divided by a sad grey *sarape*
nailed by two edges to a rafter.
There were no windows.
And in the centre of this partitioned room where the girl lay,
a loop of thick rope hung
nailed to the rafters, and it swung
lazily a few feet above a wooden stool.
It was cool in the room,
as adobe huts usually are,
but it soon began to warm
with the body heat of the women.

The moment mamá entered the hut,
señora Pozas jumped to her feet,
wringing her hands and pouring
out a torrent of incoherent words,
and obviously distressed.
But mamá's first concern was to examine the girl,
who didn't look at all pretty at that moment,
with her pain-shrunken cheeks drawn tight
like a poultice and dirty perspiration
    streaming from her.

"Ooo, doña María !" cried the woman,
    her face distraught,
"she's been having the pains all morning.
But where have you been, doña María ?
We've been waiting for you to come."

"Hot water, señora, hurry it now !"
    mamá ordered.
"I have some soap and nice clean towels."
"We sent Pepe to you this morning.
Oh doña María, what took you so long ?"
"I haven't seen Pepe today -
hot water now, ándale !"
"That Pepe! What a fool! An idiot he is!
Oh, my poor little Carmelita !"
"The water, señora, quickly if you will,
and I will light a candle,"
for it was dark and murky in the room.
"Sí, we have it already !"
exclaimed señora Pozas,
"It's boiling now - on the fire in the yard.
Juanita is helping, the good old soul.
Juanita-a! O Juanita-a !"
and the near-hysterical woman
scurried to the kitchen at the rear.

Mamá found a stub of cheap wax candle
and lit it with trembling hands
and stuck it in its own wax
on the hard-beaten earth floor.
And the yellow flickering light
managed to dispel the thick gloom,
making the room cosy like a cave.
Mamá felt the girl's pulse,
smiling warmly into her face.
Then she picked out the towel
she had soaked in water
and placed it gently
on the girl's hot brow.

"We must have you up and walking,
Carmelita," mamá said softly,
as though comforting a child
who has just had nightmares,
"it doesn't do to lie here like this.
Here, let me help you up."

"The water, doña Mariá, we have the water,"
señora Pozas said,
returning from the yard,
and she seemed less upset now
that she had something to do
and with proper assistance at hand.
She and her neighbour,
the woman named Juanita
who was a thin, unkempt thing,
carried in a large steaming pot
of water and tin basins.

"Carmelita must be walked
up and down," said mamá,
getting to her feet.

"Oh, is she a mare then ?"
señora Pozas exclaimed
with unconcious humour,
and mamá and the thin Juanita
glanced at one another,
and tried not to smile.

PART 3

"The contractions
have gone on far too long
and she's a frail little thing,"
                    mamá explained.
"Is my muchacha in danger, then -
Put the water here, Juanita, gracias."
"She'll be all right," mamá assured her,
"there's no real problem."
"Well bless the saints for that.
But, doña María, she's been asking -
she's been asking for chocolate."
"Then give her some,
or do you want the child to be born marked !"

The woman looked embarrassed,
and mamá understood at once.
"Here, Juanita," she said,
taking her purse from apron pocket
and snapping it open,
"get yourself over to the tienda
and buy two bars, ándale !"
and Juanita fled like one possessed.

"Help me walk Carmelita," mamá said,
"it's for her own good, you'll see,"
and the woman readily complied,
and the young expectant mother
was made to walk the confines of the hut,
mamá whispering encouragements
and even telling silly jokes.

Don Antonio then came in silently,
and his great height seemed incongruous
in the low-roofed hut,
and he stooped with a humble air.

His nose twitched at the chilli sharp
scent of female sweat.
He flicked large eyes over to mamá
        and solemnly nodded,
then he crept like a thief
to the other side of the partition.
Mamá heard the soft thud
as he dropped to his knees
on the close-packed dirt floor.
A cough to clear his throat,
and then he was off again praying.

The girl was allowed to lie again,
her legs drawn up.
She's so narrow, mamá observed,
glancing at the girl's thin pelvis.

Then the birth bag broke,
with a dreadful scream from the girl,
and a steaming torrent of blooded fluid
fell from her and filled the air
with a fetid stupefying odour,
and don Antonio behind the partition
stopped praying in mid-sentence,
and a soft murmur arose
from the crowd outside.

"Oh God in Heaven !" cried señora Pozas.
"Now we're well on our way," mamá said,
with an air of calm assurance.
"Help me sit her on the stool now,"
she said coolly to the señora.

Now Carmelita sat on the stool,
both her arms up and hands clutched
talonlike at the knot in the rope
hung above her head.

Don Antonio resumed praying
and Juanita returned.

A strong contraction came on
and gripped the girl like an iron fist.
She gasped and gulped for air,
her mouth open like a round black hole.
"Take it easy, muchacha," mamá soothed her,
pressing gently down on the girl's glabrous,
        distended belly,
"don't breath in like that.
Try and relax and take little breaths.
Sí, I know it is hard for you, my dear.
Press with yourself as I press...."
"Ooooh !" moaned the poor girl.
"Gently does it, good girl."
"Oh, I can't, I can't !" the girl rebelled.
"You must, my dear. I'm with you."

The air in the room was warm and humid,
with an almost animal rankness about it,
and flies flew in, torturing
the thick reeking atmosphere.
The rope was rigid as a metal rod.
Dust fell from the thatching
and the flies whined, high-pitched.

"We're almost there, muchacha."
"I can't stand it! O the pain !"
"Bear down now, my love."
"Oh mamá! Mamá-a !"
"It's coming! Oh my Carmelita !"
"Oh-my-God! I want to die !"
"There, there, my poor sweet thing."
"I want to die! To die...."
"The baby! Oh it's beautiful !"
"A girl! Well done, Carmelita !"

PART 4

       Pancho was riding
a white rawboned mare of don Roberto's,
returning from the northern boundary,
after helping with the fence repairing,
and he presently brought the mare to a halt
in the oven-hotness of a shallow gully.
He gazed unconscionably around him
under the midday sky and the flailing heat.
Then he dismounted and stretched himself,
while the mare simply dropped its head
where it stood to crop a tussock
      of dry coarse grass.

He climbed out of the gully and trod
in a powder of dust under the fierce
      noon sunlight,
then stopped and hunkered down on his heels,
and he could feel the heat burning him,
feel it drawing out sweat from his pores,
draining him of energy and the will to move.
He screwed up his seamed dark brown face
against the hard sunlight and watched
a lone hawk on the wing;
watched it soar up in the clear empty sky,
watched it describe a perfect circle
      across that immanent sky,
then it speared the eye of the sun
      and disappeared,
and he saw it no more.

Pancho sat perfectly still
over a long stretch of time,
and he could smell the dust
      and the hot stones,
        faintly aromatic;

and there was something else,
something else beside the dust
and the ubiquitous heat.....

Silence.

The harsh landscape
was still and quiet,
sagely and mysteriously
                silent,
and dead as Ishmael's plain.

The look on Pancho's face
was of a brooding sadness.
It was as if he were entirely alone
in this hot stony tract of land.
He crinkled his eyes
and wrinkled his nose,
sniffing the air.
Then he suddenly scowled
at the baking sun,
as though he had only
at this moment discovered
its hot dusty scent.

He breathed in the stony silence
through his nose and mouth
and every pore of his skin,
and his whole being
became a silence.
The rocks around him -
light-coloured angular humps
like fresh butchered
        joints of veal -
stood still in the heat,
enveloped in their own
                silence.

And even the fine sienna dust
which settled softly on the earth
    was fed by silence.

Pancho gazed at the rocks,
and he felt the heat they contained
and smelt the dust on them.
Pockmarks were holes of shadow
and the holes were like eyes
and the eyes stared blankly
at him, the earth, and the sky.

Colours changed with the play of light,
    warm desert colours;
he saw dun and ochre and orange,
burnt sienna and vermilion.
He became fully aware of the rocks,
their beauty and mystery
and authorative shapes.
Pancho felt as if he were entering
into their hard depths
and becoming a part of them.

And Pancho was at one with the rocks
    and in harmony,
and the harmony encompassed
    all the other rocks
    and all other peoples,
and the birds in the sky
and the waters of the oceans,
the mountains and the valleys,
and all things on earth.
And this was how Pancho felt
    in that deep silence,
and many moments passed.

He remained in this immovable
      rocklike state,
trapped in silence
and insufferable heat,
for quite some time.
The hardpan flat stretched
away before him,
reflecting the great sun glare.

And Pancho
dreamed
of the past....

PART 5

He dreamed of his father,
who had been a poor *peon* when Pancho
was only a boy,
eking out a miserable existence
on a stony hillside.

And Pancho dreamed of corn,
ripe rich yellow corn,
mother of mankind and sacrosanct;
and a small curving valley
up north in September,
and the peons were in the fields.
A faint wind flaking dry leaves
from the trees by a stream;
a clear bright sky,
warm and open and wide,
singing birds and busy insects,
and in the fields....
in the fields the tasseling
          golden corn.
And old man Ramírez, his father.

Ah, the seasons that came
and went for that old man.
Reap your harvest, hombre!
Aay, the husk and the seed,
the pale-stemmed straw
and the frazzled ear.
Ears of corn in the fields,
     on the hillsides,
     in the valleys;
in the sun-swept gold-washed cornlands,
in the very bosom of Mexico.

Ah! and water!.... Rain!....
        In ancient times,
before the Spaniards came to these lands,
Pancho had read at some time in his youth,
the people used to sacrifice their own kind
for the privilege of growing corn.
They had slaughtered human victims
in a barbaric orgy of hot blood,
in order to awaken Tlaloc,
their god of rain.
For the people of those times
truly believed that the seed
and the grain hears no rain
till Tlaloc has tasted
his measure of blood.

Ah sí, water and rain....
The eternal ineffaceable truth
was that corn needed rain to grow,
and the peasant who has no corn
is one who is without life.
And Pancho remembered how it was
        for his father,
remembered the cracked dusty face
        of the old man
as he looked over his parched
plot of land.

And Pancho could not help
a feeling within of something wrong
and an uncertainty about the earth
and nature and life itself,
and it gnawed at him like
rat's teeth in candlewax.
The land seemed always waterless,
sun-scarred and barren.
The dry soil crumbled
        into lifeless dust,

and the hot winds would come
        and lift the dust
and throw it mockingly
over the sunbaked hills and fields.
Even hardy plants withered
and died in the hard splintered earth,
and age-old trees wilted
and bled tears of sorrow
from wounds of cracked bark.

And old man Ramírez used to stand
by his meagre plot and gaze
for interminable periods of time
across that devastation
of arid clods of earth,
and in his eyes would be seen
a soul-tearing eloquence
of misery and hopelessness;
and Pancho had observed
these bitter realities
like a melancholy Marius
haunting the ruins of Carthage....

A hot searing wind
suddenly rose in the west,
dust and grit riding the wind,
and Pancho at once looked up.
He felt the hard heat upon him
as he stood up and lowered his eyes,
resting them on a thorn tree
miraculously growing from a crack
        in the hardpan flat.

Pancho's eyes flicked
from the thorn tree,
and he suddenly started
from his brooding reverie.

His eyes rounded in alarm
for there in the heat shimmer
was a small gnarled figure trotting
with short, rapid steps
over the hardpan flat;
dressed in filthy dusty rags,
back bent forward against the wind
and the weight of a large bundle
     of driftwood.
To Pancho, it was as if the man
had sprung out from
the very bowels of the earth.

Papá! The old hombre!
was Pancho's first incredible thought.
What's he doing here ?
eyes glued in wonder on the apparition
agilely skipping across the flat,
wind-flown dust swirling around it.

PART 6

The figure came nearer,
and all at once Pancho laughed
with sudden relief,
for he recognised who it was -
Santo, the pueblo's oldest citizen.

"Oye, Santo !" he called over huskily.
"Que pasó, hombre ?"
"Corncob !" returned the man agedly,
twisting his dark wizened face
sideways under his load. "What is it ?
What's the matter ?"

"Why nothing, you old stump !"
Pancho laughed,
"but what are you doing out here ?
Ah well, I can see well enough
what you're about,
but it's a hot one, isn't it ?
Ay qué caray, the only thing growing
out here is the damned heat, hmm."

"How right, Corncob, he-he !"
chuckled the old man,
and he stopped and waited
for the other to join him,
bouncing up and down all the while
on his knotted limbs.

"Well, how goes it, amigo ?"
Pancho asked,
looking into the ancient's
black beady eyes;
like a cock's
hard and glintingly cunning.

His face was a mesh
of fine brown wrinkles
and he was toothless.

"Muy bien, very good !
But where's your horse ?"
and the old man followed
        Pancho's nod.
"Hum, in the gully, is it ?
And you're here, why ?
What are you up to, hey ?"
and the old man sniffed,
his eyes boring into Pancho.

"Nothing, you old stick.
Just back from fence repairing."
"Don't see any fencing around here,"
Santo said with a sly wink.
"Up at the northern boundary,"
        Pancho explained,
"Roberto's land, you coyote."

And at that moment the wind
suddenly died down
and the air became still again,
hot and choked with dust.
"The wind's dropped," Pancho said.
"Sí, as it must," quipped the ancient.
"Strange weather...."
"It's a sign, Corncob,
that's what it is, he-he !"

Then Santo jumped to a subject
        more to his liking:
"Well, do you have a drop of mezcal
then ? I'm afire with thirst."
"No, my friend," Pancho said.
"Not a drop ? That's bad, that is,"

Santo spat, skipping nimbly
with the heavy load of wood
strapped to his back
and incapable of staying still
for even an instant,
moving about on his feet
in a half jogging fashion.

"Well, Santo, what goes on
        in the pueblo,
for I know you for a nosy old stick
and get in everywhere, aay hmm."
"That's me to a turn, he-he !
because I'm sharp, I am,"
Santo winked craftily.
He poked a twig of a finger at dust
in the corner of his eye,
and winked again with the other eye
rather slyly, then said:
"Ah hum, you know the Pozas girl -
what's her name ? - Carmelita ?"
"Hm'm, I know the muchacha."
"Well, she'll drop today."
"Now how can you say that ?"
        Pancho laughed.
"I just said it, he-he !"
"But how can you know, eh ?"
"I know because I'm old and wise,
and I know who seeded her too !"
Santo said with malignant glee,
hopping with agility on one foot
to the other with utter restlessness.
"We all know that," Pancho countered.

"Well, I'm on my way now, I am,"
Santo said abruptly with a grimace.
"Out of my way there!
Let a man pass, will you ?

All this open space around here,
and you have to park
your damned hide in front of me.
I'll see you when I see you
and not a minute before.
I'm off ! I'm off *pronto*
and you can't stop me, he-he-he !"

And at last old Santo's restless
movements propelled him forward,
and off he went, at that half-trot
perculiar to Mexican peasants,
who prefer to travel that way
even with a load on their backs.

"*Vámanos*, Santo ! Adíos, Corncob !"
he called over his shoulder.
"Adíos, hombre ! Adíos !"
and Pancho watched him go
with a helpless grin on his face.
He lifted his sombrero
and scratched his scalp,
his livid ginger hair stood
up like a stiff brush.
He hawked and spat on the hot
        rock of the flat,
then returned to the gully
        to mount his horse.

Pancho urged on the mare,
and the horse snorted with the stinging dust
        and kicked up its heels.
It set off across the hardpan flat
        at a hurried walk,
hooves clipping hollowly on the rock.
While old Santo soon became a dot
in the shimmering distance,
like a worker ant carrying a dead fly.

Book Three

"Afternoon"

PART 1

A tangible air
of excitement pervaded the Ramos' homestead,
an atmosphere of festive chaos
so prevalent among Mexican families.

Mamá appeared to be fussing and fretting
about the hearth,
trying to do more than two jobs at once,
or so it seemed.
Her small brigade of incompetents,
namely Christina, Ruth and Julia,
helpful cooks, maybe, but decidedly
in the way of mamá's culinary progress.
But mamá's main cause of fretfulness
was the fact that their guest,
sénor Francisco Ramírez - or Pancho,
had not yet showed his face on the farm,
and so there was a slight delay.

Juan stood idly by, watching
with a male detatched interest
as the four females bustled
feverishly at the homely ritual
of preparing food for the family.
And the dog found no interest at all
in the culinary goings-on,
a rare attitude of mind indeed;
perhaps it was bothered by the heat.
It was sound asleep under the shade
of a wooden bench,
hard by his master's feet,
floppy ragged ears twitching at flies.

"There's too much grease in the soup,"
Christina remarked, stirring a pot
on the crackling fire.

"You think so ?" mamá said.
"Well, you may be right,
but don't stir it in so,"
for mamá was the expert.
"I'll skim it, mamá."
"Sí, please do that,
but after it's settled."

Ruth was frying tacos, giving them
an exceedingly dark brown appearance,
and Julia was doing nothing in particular
except getting under mamá's feet.
"The beans are going to boil over !"
Julia cried, all of a tremble.
"Oh mamá. the beans are coming up !"
"They're doing alright, my *niña* -
Ruth, that's enough for now,"
as mamá's eyes rested with misgiving
on the pile of darkly brown tacos.
"Sí, mamá," said Ruth, and mamá sighed.

The battle continued to rage
around the kitchen fire:
"A lemon, Ruth, if you please," asked mamá.
"These onions smell strong," said Ruth,
chopping away with tears in her eyes.
"Mamá wants a lemon, Ruth,"
        Christina reminded her.
"Now where's the *nopal* I washed ?" said mamá.
"What is it you want, mamá ?" said Ruth.
"Mamá wants a lemon, Rutí," said Christina.
"My nopal," mamá said. "It's all right,
        I'm only talking to myself,
as I usually do - you know my ways,"
        she laughed merrily.

"Ruth, cut this for me, will you ?"

"Here's the nopal I was looking for.
I'll get this on the go -
Chihuahua ! but it's hot today."
"You're on top of the fire, mamá,
please let me do that."
"I'm managing well, thank you."
"The *tamales* look ready - Ruth ?"
"More wood ! I must have more wood,
my fire's going out !"
"I'll get it, mamá."
"Thank you, Julia my love."
"Ruth,you didn't cut the -"
"Oh, the pot ! The pot !"
"I've got it, don't panic."
"Ruth, can't you move a little faster ?"
"Leave me be, Christina, por favor."
"Stop it now, you two !"
"I'll do this myself, thank you !
"Sí, you do that !"
"*Gracias* !"
"*De nada* !"
"O hum-hum-hum, te-hum-hum-hum !"
          sang mamá happily,
fully in the spirit of things.
"Oh mamá," laughed Ruth,
"you sound so funny !"
"This tastes real good,
how did you make it, mamá ?"
"Excuse me, Christina -
Oh, these twigs prick !"
"Just put them on the fire, Rutí."
"hum-hum, te-te-hum-hum !"

There was then a great thudding
of hooves and all heads turned
in the direction of the sound.

PART 2

       Pancho himself hove in sight,
riding in on don Roberto's mare
which was looking rather the worse for wear.

"Hola ! my friends, it's only me,"
Pancho greeted them blithely,
raising his sombrero high
and describing circles of salutation.

"Señor Ramírez ! Pancho ! Pancho !"
the children chorused
with great enthusiasm.
"And about time too,"
said mamá under her breath,
chuckling away to herself.
"Now things will get started !"
she fancied, eyeing the old ranchero.
And Juan was up from his seat
     like a grasshopper
       to attend to the horse,
and Julia skipped swiftly to Pancho.

"Oh señor Ramírez ! *Hurra* !" she cried,
and her eyes were happily gleaming,
as she flung herself at him
and hugged his bandy legs.
"Ho-ho ! My little sun-blossom !"
     laughed Pancho, chucking her cheek.
"Why, ay qué caray, if you're not
the loveliest creature for mile's around,
then I'm a dirty dog's ear ˙
and I would never lie !"
"But I am !" smiled Julia sweetly,
with that naïve self-confidence
     of the very young.

Mamá, her arms slack by her side,
stared wonderstruck at Pancho's
incredibly dusty appearance
for he was covered in it
from the crown of his sombrero
    to his feet.
"Well !" she exclaimed with a hearty laugh,
"You do look a sight, Pancho.
Been playing with the hogs, or what ?"

"Something like that, María,"
    roared Pancho,
and he whipped his sombrero off
and sunlight set ablaze
his thatch of ginger hair.
"We had a little stampede, you see -
And how goes it with my own
    little bush-flower, hmm ?"
bending down to Julia.

"A stampede !" mamá cried. "Merciful heavens!
and what next, might I ask ?
There's always something or other
when you're around, you rogue !"
"The herd stampeded ?" asked Juan,
    eyes round in surprise.
"What's a stampede ?" Julia wanted to know.

"Sí," said Pancho, "that damn fool -
excuse me - that nephew idiot
of don Roberto's - What's his name? -
Sergio, he let off a pistol
in the middle of the cattle
and gave us all a merry run, hm-m."

"Ahh, that Sergio," said Juan,
and he took the white mare by the rein
and led her off to the stable,

as don Antonio emerged from his room
to welcome the guest.

"Chihuahua !" said mamá. "Was anyone hurt ?"
"Well, Mario went arse over tit.
Fell from his horse and lost his shirt
- but we all survived," Pancho chuckled.
"Lost his shirt ?"
and mamá puzzled over that one.

"But you, señor Ramírez," said Ruth,
open-eyed and passionately attentive,
"are you okay ?"
"Me ?" grinned Pancho. "Them beasts
ran all over me, but what harm
can they do to me, h'mm ?
Apart from chewing a kilo of dust,
        I'm fine, real fine !"
and he went to mamá, took her hand
        and tenderly kissed it.

"Pfoo ! you stink like a skunk,"
mamá recoiled from him.
"I am a skunk, believe it.
Well María, am I too late ?
If so, just throw me a bone
and I'll chew on that, uuy !"
"You can clean up first," mamá said,
"you look as if you live in a burrow."
"I'll just bury my head
in the horse trough," he winked.
"You'll do no such thing, you rascal !"
mamá's podgy arms akimbo
on her ample hips. "Ruth,
a bucket of hot water and soap
for the señor here, por favor."
"Carambas !" said Pancho, "I have to wash ?"

"Chihuahuas !" mamá burst out.
"Okay, okay, I'll go wash, if you insist,"
and they both began to laugh,
with heads held back,
eyes screwed and crinkled.

Pancho savoured the delicious cooking
    aromas wafting his way.
He slapped his dusty sombrero
against his thigh, then coughed and spat
in the smoke of dust he had created.

Don Antonio stepped forward then,
and he towered over Pancho,
who looked up at him,
comradely grinning.
Don Antonio faintly smiled,
    stooped fractionally,
    and they shook hands.
"How goes it then, *compadre* ?"
"Muy bien, Pancho, and you ?"
"Hungry, hombre," winked Pancho.
"I could eat a whole steer."
"Is the herd safe ?" asked don Antonio,
being as it were indirectly
    reminded of it.
"Sí, tucked in the canyon they are,
all watered down, and licking
dust off their hides, bless them,"
and Pancho rose and fell on his toes
and heels and stretched his arms
to ease his small aches and pains.

About to hawk and spit, as was his habit,
he stopped himself in time,
as mamá confronted him.
"Here, wash yourself," she ordered
with warm and open brusqueness,

154

handing him water and soap and a towel.
"Right ! right !" he shouted
with rugged cheerfulness.
He sluiced his hands and arms,
splashed and spluttered as he dunked
his head in the bucket,
slapped dust from himself
    and washed again.
As he dried himself
and dirtied the towel in the process,
he inhaled the aroma of food
and winked at mamá shamelessly.
Ruth and Julia watched him
intently, cracking *pepita* seeds
all the while with their teeth.

Juan returned from the stable
and gazed admiringly at his hero:
    Pancho *el ranchero*;
tough but warm-hearted,
strong, solid, dependable;
old and honest and wise.
And very special to Juan.

The broad sunlight brought out
the barbaric ruggedness
of the old man's features,
deepened the weathered criss-cross
of lines on his cheeks and brow,
and struck silvery gleams of light
in the irises of his merry blue eyes.
And there was that ever ready expression
of simple humour on his open face.

Then mamá clapped her hands,
a signal for everyone to sit,
    and quickly or else....

PART 3

        Mamá worked furiously
on the last minute cooking,
refusing help from anyone
for this her supreme moment.
The heat from the fire flushed
her face red-brown
and sweat dropped from her.
The pots and jugs on the fire
        bubbled and sang,
wreathed in steam and smoke.
This inestimable lady worked
        like a furnace stoker,
putting the fuel of her motherly
love into the task at hand.

Pancho sat four-square; that is,
slowly and surely crushing
the flimsy reed chair under him.
He wiggled about precariously,
ready at any moment
to land on the ground.
He turned his head, sniffing
the kitchen smells like a starved dog;
and in fact his belly was growling.

He was almost ready to shove
a finger up his nose - the finger
wavered uncertainly below his nostril
- remembered in time what he was about,
and sniffed again instead, briefly,
with a perculiar air of significance.
Then he turned his head back
and grinned and shrugged at don Antonio
with devil-may-care nonchalance,
winked and nodded and smiled kindly

down on the children,
and accepted from Julia the tiniest hand
of the *calabaza* seeds called *pepitas*.
The seeds, he soon found,
were simply a tease,
for he could not crack them
as expertly as the girls,
and the thin shells stuck
to the back of his mouth
like fragments of glass.
Julia was about to offer him more
but was checked by a faint frown
which appeared on her papá's face.

The dog woke up and seemed of a sudden
very attentive, very ravenous,
and very vexed when nothing came of it.
And Juan draped a *poncho*
over the parrot's cage,
to discourage the bird from screaming
abuse at everyone, as it so often did
when the family gathered for comida.

Sunlight slipped through the shade trees
and dappled with gold the unusually silent
        diners at the wooden table.
In the centre of the table was placed
        a squat fruit jar,
from the wide neck of which reposed
a bunched colourful variety of flowers
picked by Julia from mamá's own garden.
And motes of dust like tiny bright bugs
danced on the air in the sunlight.
The curiously subdued group at the table,
in order to hide their awkward silence,
took a curious intensity of interest
at a trio of hens ruffling their feathers
        in the dust of the yard.

Don Antonio's time had come.
He coughed to clear his throat,
quickly glanced around him,
and solemnly intoned a brief prayer
of thanks for the food
they were about to receive,
then all made a sign of the cross
with hurried, impatient motions.

What could be safely described
as pandimonium then broke
        loose at the table.
Everyone began talking at once,
Pancho's rasping voice and rough
turn of speech predominant.
There was a clatter of dishes
and whisps of steam curling
at each place setting, and poor mamá
was running like a scalded cat
to and fro between hearth and table.
Don Antonio lordly splashed
a generous mugful of *pulque*
for Pancho from a tin mug,
and Christina poured hot lemon-grass
tea from a chipped enamel pot
into cups for herself and the children.

The family set to vociferously
with eyes and teeth and fingers,
putting a blizzard of energy
into eating and talking,
while mamá watched over them
with a widening smile
of immeasurable satisfaction;
blissful sounds indeed to her,
the munching and the chewing
and the crunching, the champing
of busy teeth and jaws jogging,

        gulping, swallowing -
a gastronomic symphony.

"This weather is never going to break,"
don Antonio remarked as his opening
piece of conversation to his guest.
"But it usually does," quipped Pancho,
his swarthy face dipped to his dish,
snorting over chicken *caldo*,
and don Antonio's brows met
        in a slight frown,
as though he was vexed at something.
"That drought of last year,
and nothing wet to show this year,"
he went on with a gloomy air.
"The corn stores are low now -"
"It'll rain soon enough, amigo,
we'll have it in barrelfuls,"
and Pancho looked quizzically asquint
up at the bright blue of the sky
as if his thoughts hung there;
then more important things came to mind,
and down went his head again,
slurping in his soup.

"More pulque ?" offered don Antonio.
"Ah sí, thank you," Pancho thanked
him warmly, "I could do with a wet."
He raised his bowl to his lips
and noisily slurped the broth.
He wiped his lips and moustache
        with his sleeve; then,
with arms resting on the table,
he cupped his pulque with both hands
as if it were holy sacrament.

"Eat up there," mamá told him,
"rice and chillies under your nose,
hot tacos here with spinach -
Chihuahuas ! all this food lying
around untouched,"
she admonished him.
"Ah sí, María, I'm ready for it."
"Get on with it, then," mamá said,
and Pancho picked up a taco,
face taking on a look of a starveling
about to devour a stolen chicken.

Juan was whispering to Ruth,
and Ruth looked up and suddenly asked:
"Is it true, señor Ramírez,
that you rode with the famous
        Pancho Villa ?"
"Sí, is it true ?" said Juan.

PART 4

    Ruth's mild brown eyes
glanced shyly down the table at Pancho,
and she smiled briefly and blushingly,
    showing white teeth.
"Who's he ?" Julia wanted to know.
"Well now, I may be an old man, hmm,"
    said Pancho,
filtering his words
through a mouthful of food,
"but I was only as young as you now
    in his bandit days. Hmm."

He glanced sideways at Juan
and thought he saw disappointment there,
and said: "A cousin of mine
    was with him though,"
and the desired effect seemed to work.
"A *dorado* ?" Juan asked eagerly,
    his face lighting up.
"Sí, one of - what's his name ? -
one of Villa's dorados,
and surrendered with him
to Obregón in ....oh, 1920."
"Who is Obregón ?" chimed in Julia.
"Why, he was the *presidente*
at that time, my bush-flower."

"That's interesting," said Juan,
"about Villa, I mean."
"Sí, and three years later he got
himself killed. Assassinated. H'mm."
"Assassinated, what is that ?"
    Julia wormed in again.
"Your cousin was killed ?" said Ruth,
picking a fly out of her tea.

"No, Villa, Pancho Villa."
"Who did it ? Who killed him ?"
"Why the *federales* of course.
Uuy, they had no trust in him, you see.
But, carajo ! what a man he was."

"He was a bandit," put in mamá,
"Just like you Pancho, you rascal !"
"A bandit !" Juan grinned at Pancho.
"He's a ranchero," said Ruth.
"It's much the same thing," said mamá,
smiling down on Pancho
who was fluffing up with pride.
He blew out his cheeks,
expanded his chest
- the reed chair creaked alarmingly -
squinted his eyes and villainously
grinned at all around him.
"Some more pulque ?" said don Antonio.
"Ah thanks, compadre."
"Well, Pancho, *salud*."
"Salud !"
and the drink went down very well
        in Pancho's estimation.

The family talked and ate on
in a general mood of well-being,
hands continually flapping at the flies.
Julia tittered to herself
behind the cover of a tortilla,
as she watched the steady progress
of a fly sucking at chicken grease
dribbling down Pancho's jaw.
He tore a leg to pieces
and noisily chomped away.
He sucked and gnawed on the bone,
meat and sinew sliding
between his teeth and tongue.

164

Mamá hovered by, her eyes watchful
and her manner attentive,
secretly astonished and pleased
at Pancho's voracious appetite;
she clasped her hands before her
and bounced on her heels with pleasure.

A warm fresh chorale of birdsong
entertained the family gathering,
in harmony with the music from the pueblo,
which could be distinctly heard.
"Some more pulque, Pancho ?"
"Sí, compadre, gracias."
And don Antonio almost grinned,
but settled instead for a weak smile,
as Pancho cleared food debris
from between his teeth
and smacked his lips.
"Salud !" he said,
and down gushed the pulque.

Don Antonio poured again
with solemn graciousness,
while mamá fetched fresh dishes of food
and put them before the ranchero,
and Pancho ate and stuffed
        and crammed his mouth,
near choked himself on pulque
as he chugged it down,
moustache white with froth.
He loudly belched,
to everyone's approval.

"Try these meat tamales," urged mamá.
"Papacito, you're slow today,"
and she put her hand affectionately
on her husband's shoulder.

"Rutí, just look at señor Ramírez !"
Julia sniggered artlessly,
nudging her sister in the side.
"Look at his hair all sticking up !"
"Sí, and like it's on fire."
"His ears are jumping up and down."
"And his moustache is all white !"
"Oh I shall laugh if I look again -"
"And what are you two chuntering at ?"
mamá asked, suddenly appearing
behind the girls and wagging her head.
"It was nothing, mamá," said Ruth.
"Well, eat up now, and be good."

Pancho nonchalantly tossed a nub
of cheese into his mouth
and washed it down with pulque.
A wasp settled on his tamale
and Ruth kindly reached across
and gently fanned it away.
"More pulque ?" don Antonio asked
his guest with splendid dignity.
"Ah sí, por favor. I was wondering
if you were going to hog it all,"
Pancho joked.
"Gracias, muchas gracias. Salud !"
and don Antonio mildly smiled.

The table was by now a devastation.
A litter of torn pieces of tortilla,
shreds of onion and chicken,
chicken bones and gristle,
squeezed lemons, chilli and tomato seeds.

Swarms of ugly black flies
zeroed down on the table.
The entire family chattered
gaily like sparrows,
and Pancho was getting more tipsy,
merry and loquacious
by the minute....

PART 5

"There was a time
up Durango way once - " Pancho
was saying to Juan,
after first throwing a quick
wary glance at don Antonio
out of the corner of his eye.
"A fresh tamale, Christina ?"
"Sí, gracias, mamá."
"I'm feeling full," said Julia.
"Me too," agreed Ruth.
"Can I leave, mamá ?"
"You just stay put, niña !"
" - and this nosy priest
came along," Pancho continued,
touching Juan's knee and winking,
"and this priest, he says to me:
'Well señor, and how long
have you been working here ?'
Well, chocala ! I looks up at the sun
and then at the priest,
and I says to him:
' Oh, it must be getting on
for three hours now, padre,'"
and Pancho threw back his head
and rolled off a great
            bellowing guffaw.

Don Antonio was hard put to it
to maintain his usual dignity.
He idly wondered if his guest's
evident jocularity stemmed from some
natural source in his personality,
or was perhaps the result
of drinking too much pulque,
he couln't decide which.

And then a moment later,
the popular *El Cuartelazo*
started up in the pueblo,
the lively bouncy *corrido*
sounding loud and clear
over the heads of the family
gathering, and Pancho
could not have been presented
with a better moment.
With the most surprising agility
he went cat-wise to Ruth
and whisked the girl from her stool.

"A dance ! Dance !" he cried,
holding her hand in his great fist
and leading her away from the table.
"Oho !" mamá laughed, and then told
Christina to go fetch her guitar.

Pancho stood like a monument over Ruth.
He raised his long arms high
and smartly clapped his hands.
"*Ahua* !" he cried the cry of Mexico,
and his spatula paws enclosed
Ruth's rounded shoulders,
and they began to dance.

Pancho's left foot slewed across the dust
and slapped into his right, a stomp,
then the right foot skimmed
over to meet the other - stomp !
Then round and round they went
with the dust boiling up
around their knees.
His ungainly figure spun dizzily,
revolving around Ruth with jerks
of his massive shoulders.

Meantime Christina returned with the guitar
and her expert fingers began swiftly
 tuning the strings,
 then started playing,
creating a lively atmosphere of gaiety.
And the dance really got under way,
as Pancho stomped his feet,
raising clouds of dust.
"Ahua !" he roared,
lifting himself springily
 like a playful bear,
whirling and pivoting
round and round Ruth,
while the family beat time
by clapping their hands
or banging on the table:
Clap !- clap !- clap !- clap ! -"Ahua !"
and up came the knees,
 up came the dust.
Julia's face was a study in ecstatic
irrepressible delight as she followed
the movements of the dancers
with gay sparkling eyes.
And she soon realised that she was not
herself in the limelight,
which needed putting right at once.
So, on a daring impulse,
the tenderling bobbed up from her stool,
and, catching the contagious
 gaiety of the melody,
 she tapped a *zapateado*,
 the Spanish tap dance.
And she did it remarkably well,
with dust spuming up around her
as she smacked the earth
 with her tiny feet.
Her eyes sought the table
to see if her efforts were duly

appreciated, and indeed they were.
Mamá wagged her head encouragingly
and Julia gained confidence from this
and her little feet pattered faster,
with such inexpressible naturalness.

Christina thumped away at the strings
as if her very life depended on it;
and the dog nosed purposely
        toward a tempting bone
        lying near Pancho's feet,
then hastily backed away
        as Pancho turned,
its paws padding in amazing time
        to the music.

"A-ahua ! A-ahua !" cried Pancho,
and the beat was even faster now
with quickening strains
        of the music.
"Pick your feet up, Pancho !"
        laughed mamá,
"or you'll drill yourself
        into the ground."
"Can't help it, María !"
Pancho bellowed over from a storm of dust,
as though he was on the range
        and driving cattle,
"weighed down with food I am !"
"Pulque, more like, I'm thinking,"
        retorted mamá.
"I've had enough of that
and this dancing," puffed Pancho,
and he quit there and then,
        just as the music did.

Book Four

"Evening"

PART 1

      Pancho had left
the Ramos' homestead a few hours before
and was now, like many another ranchero,
in search of some peace and quiet.
He followed a beaten track leading
to a bend in the river named Sancho's Elbow.
On his right was a cornfield,
sunbaked, stony and stubbly;
on his left a narrow olive-green belt
of *carrizos*, and beyond that
the valley's near-dry riverbed.
The path led to a wood
of scrub oak and mesquite.
A hot wind was blowing from the northwest,
and the trees, casting long shadows,
stirred with a dry rustling sound,
like the rapids of a young river.
The sundried grass whispered raspingly,
and his head passed through a cloud
of midges frantically living out
            their last hour.

He was soon into a clearing
where the river behind the trees
      took a sharp turn.
This was Sancho's Elbow.
It was no more than three hundred
      paces or so south
of the ruined walls of el castillo.
Pancho sat himself down on a fallen tree
blown down by a past storm,
his bandy legs casually stretched out
straight in front of him,
sombrero pushed to the back of his head.

The sun had now lowed,
its last red rays splintering
the trees, and the shadows
stretched long over the glade.
There was a high whine of mosquitoes,
a dark mist of them
came from the stagnant pools
of the riverbed at Sancho's Elbow.
And there was a chirrup
of grasshoppers in the grasses,
and an all-pervading reek
        of dried river mud.
And Pancho's eyes narrowed
as he faced the red glare
        of the westering sun.

The light was dying in the east
with the evening's imperative force
sucking the sun down
toward the mountains.
The western sky turned
from cerulean to amethyst;
and in that sky was a long solitary
smear of blooded cloud tapered
to a point like a spear.
And there was a screeching
of many birds fighting for places
to roost for the night
on the carrizo fronds.

Pancho absently scratched himself,
gazed again at the setting sun
with a preoccupied air.
The sun painted the hills gold
and el castillo blazed
in brilliant light,

the sun molten on the crowns
    of the trees,
where many birds
were chapping and chipping.

Pancho heard a burro blasting
    off in the valley,
and the mournful howling
of a stray dog up on the hill
        beyond the wood.
        A cock crowed
        then another.
He was concious of the
changing evening colours;
the burnished rose hills
glowed warmly in the gaps
        of the trees,
the trees set aflame by the seething
crimson orb of the sun,
and lilac-washed the mountains now
    as the falling sun
    neared the cordillera.

Pancho got up and stood in the light
of the setting sun cutting
through the tree branches.
He looked between the trees
at the livid red sun
wounding the hills,
the rocks shadow-lidded
    and silent.
There were gold and purple tints
splashed on the distant cordilllera.
And Pancho twisted his moustache,
    pulled and tugged at it,
    as if inwardly agitated.

PART 2

The sun had set.

The sun was now invisible
behind the mountain range,
but its glow was still in the sky.
The mountains were plum purple,
with a moody maroon trim of foothills,
in this soft evening light,
this last dying light of the day.
Flocks and colonies of birds
chittered in the trees
and swaying carrizos.
The chapel bell struck
        in the pueblo
and its sound travelled
the length of the valley
        and up the hills.

And the mountains darkened now,
showing a face the colour
        of spiced cider,
        then purple-black,
and darkening even more.
The dusk came down,
a purple-blue dusk
which steadily deepened,
and in that gathering dusk
Pancho went soft-footed,
and the tide of dusk rolled
in quietly with him
as he padded soundlessly
between bush and shrubbery.

Soft dusk.
It came over from beyond the hills
and mountains in the east,
crept over smotheringly
like the slow folding
of a light blanket,
in the shadows of silence,
in the coming darkness
        of a young night.
And Pancho stopped for a moment,
for with the deepening gloom
came a mist such as he had
never seen or known before,
vaporous and phantasmal,
and he felt in the air
the first bold strength
        of night.

The long accumulated heat
of the day was coming out
of the stones and grasses
        of the earth,
rising up in small waves,
hot draughts of air,
stirring the dry crisp
leaves of the trees.

The first stars came out one by one,
glittering and winking above him,
        in the darkling night sky.
Pancho's whole being was aware
of nature's daily transformations
when day becomes night,
and in doing so and all at once
        he trembled,
then the trembling ceased,
        and he listened.

180

Around him crickets sang
their monotonous evening-song,
    and a small bat,
out from some dark nook
of the ancient monastery
    of el castillo,
zinged closely and alarmingly
    by his ear.
    Mosquitoes whined.
There was a brief scutter
    of a tiny animal,
probably a field mouse,
in the long honey gold grass,
now dark and mysterious.
And other unidentifiable
noises in this thickening
    darkness of night.

        Then silence....

PART 3

> There was a featherlight
stillness in the air,
a deep and unearthly quietness.
Pancho wondered at this silence
> all around him.
It seemed so strange, and gave him
an eerie feeling, made him cold.

The birds had quietened of a sudden,
> they made not a murmur.
And insects stopped their normal
incessant chirring and buzzing.
There was not a rustle of leaf
> or blade of grass.
There was only the silence.

And Pancho scratched his shank
with nervous puzzlement.

> And then
> there came a fearful
continuous expanding roar
> of sound,
like the oncoming of an express train.
Cat-eyed, Pancho glanced through
the semidarkness at the pueblo
> across the river,
but the village was now gone,
lost in a towering, monstrous,
> boiling whirlwind.
"*Tremolino* !" gasped Pancho.

It swept across the valley
in a matter of seconds,
veered round in an instant,

then pounced on him
with a shattering force.
He watched fascinated as the trees
bent before the powerful wind,
creaked and groaned with strain.
The whirlwind swallowed him,
his ears near bursting
with the thundrous roar.
And he was lashed by flying debris
of straw, broken branches,
        grit and stones.

Pancho dropped to the ground,
tried to bury himself in the earth,
his hair whipped and matted
with whirling dust and debris.
And the wind shrieked horribly.
The air was in a ferment;
turgid, heavy with dust
and flying fragments.
A tree nearby to him
was suddenly uprooted,
and fell with an appalling crash.
He seemed as if he were slowly choking,
lungs bursting, eyes stinging
        with biting dust.

And the wind howled frenziedly,
churning up a maelstrom of thick,
        clogging dust and earth.
It struck a nearby empty hut,
a black swirling cloud of destruction.
It took off the reed cane roof -
- the roof lifted ponderously
and slewed off into the air.
The timber rafters strained,
splintered and cracked,
and away went the beams and
thatching, flung far afield.

And the hut no longer existed.

The whirlwind passed,
spun on south down the valley,
left a great dark pall
of smoking dust and devastation.

And then, of a sudden
there was a great flash
of light in the sky.
Then there was one long
deafening explosion
        of thunder,
like a crack of doom,
and the earth trembled.

Another dazzling light
flashed in the sky,
lighting the whole valley.
Another loud crash
        of thunder,
followed by a stutter
of heavy raindrops
on the tree branches.
A cutting blast of wind
swept through the glade.

Pancho felt the splashes of
                water
on his face and he was greatly amazed.
        "*Rain* !"
        he croaked
in the booming of the wind.

PART 4

Pancho got to his feet.
A curious sensation gripped him.
And another clap of thunder broke,
        went rolling away,
reverberating over the entire
        valley and beyond.

The stormhead advanced,
let loose its vengeance.
Lightning flashed again,
thunder cracked and rumbled,
rain drummed and lashed.
The windshaken trees bowed
in homage to the hard-driven
        nails of rain,
a crushing heavy ceaseless torrent
plunking into the earth
like machine-gun fire.

A crashing bolt of lightning
suddenly struck the monastery;
there was a thunderous boom,
masonry split and toppled,
rocks and chunks of mortar
thrown out in a blasting explosion.
And fire erupted from the bowels
        of the monastery,
flames leaping from the ancient
cells and passageways.
And Pancho's eyes bulged,
pinned to the flames
roaring up from the blistered
depths of the monastery,
a blazing inferno of hell.

And the thunder continued
to roll right overhead
as Pancho blinked his eyes,
gazing awestruck at the burning monastery,
orange-red flames spitting and crackling,
consuming agèd timbers and musty dust.
A vein in his throat throbbed,
as another sudden rip of thunder
burst right over his head.

Pancho's clothes were now soaked
through with the wind-driven rain.
Lightning flared, the thunder rumbled,
and the wind boomed and whistled.
The trees crackled and rustled
          in their branches,
weeping great tears of rain.
The wind cried too in the trees,
as the thunder rolled
          unceasingly overhead.
And the wind-flown rain angled
horizontally against Pancho's body.

A seething torrential downpour
          was sheeting on him.
The glade was a churned mire
          of slush and thick oily mud.
The earth's parched flesh
drank in the slime in rippling gulps,
the floodwater gushing like a weir.
Loose leaves scudded with the wind,
and harder came the rain,
a slashing, pelting rain.
And the lighning lit the evening sky
          and the thunder crashed
                    and rolled.

And then, all in a moment,
a rocket flare shot
into the evening sky
and exploded with a loud crack.
Campesinos were out
on a drunken rampage.
Dark figures crashed gleefully
through the tall reed grass
on the river bank,
calling to one another
in excitable voices
from the wet shadows.
"The river's rising !"
they shouted joyfully.
"Ayí, how it runs !"

Kerosene flares bobbed and waved
        along the river bank,
firecrackers barked and spat
        in the rain-soaked shadows.
The campesinos yelled
and whooped with delight,
tore their way through
a web-dripping frieze
of leaves and rain.

And they squelched off
        into the night,
calling and laughing
        all the while,
greatly thankful and relieved
that the long dry season
        had at last broken.

            And at last that dust
            was laid to rest.

PART 5

The wind dropped.

There was a steady rain falling,
     a wet mist of rain,
     soft and clinging,
     tenuous, gentle
     and caressing.
And this mist of rain closed in
and clamped its raintraced
dankness on Pancho in the glade.

He listened to the dull beating
     of the rain,
floodwater burbling
and frothing around him.
And the rain was falling
softly now, a fine drizzle.
A ribbon of water fell
from a tree branch
and scattered drops dripped
down his neck.
And there were still occasional
flails of lightning
and thunder growling
     in the distance
as the storm moved on.

Pancho decided he would head back
toward the Ramos farmstead,
in order to pick up the mare
and return it to don Roberto.
And so he tramped and gimped
slowly and purposely through
a roil of muddy rainwater,
a clammy saturine morass.

And as Pancho moved on,
feet squelching in the muddied earth,
his thoughts turned
to the Ramos girls;
and to a time past
- late spring two years before -
when he had found them in a field,
    picking wildflowers.

He had himself felt intoxicated
by the many wildflowers;
    by their colours
    and their beauty
        and scents.
And he had stood and watched
the two girls picking flowers
under a warm and gentle
    late spring sun.

There had seemed a timeless
atmosphere of coziness
in that lazy afternoon warmth,
when the things of nature
created innumerable little miracles.
The girls ran knee-deep through
a thick rich carpet of flowers,
picking them by the handful,
tender-eyed and laughing
for no reason at all
except perhaps for sheer joy
of life and living.

And the flowers were all around them,
a multitudinous riot of living colour.
And not only wild flowers.
There were lavender and purple asters,
white baby's breath, tiny and fine,

192

red cockscombs and yellow daisies,
        and bright orange marigolds.
All waving with the corn,
smothering the afternoon air
with their fragrant perfumes.
And the two girls gathered
these flowers by the armful,
calling to each other
and continually bursting
into gleeful laughter.

While the *milperos* toiled
in the valley's broad belt of fields;
ground squirrels dared to chatter
among thickets of thorn in blossom,
scampering up the trunks
of beefwood and mesquite.
A light honey gold haze swam
in quiet splendour over the
cerulean expanse of sky.

And the girls romped through fields
of white and yellow daisies
and sweet marigolds and dandilions
- a cloth of old Aztec gold
spread richly over the land....

And Pancho's thoughts
drifted on aimlessly
as the soft rain fell
        about him.

EPILOGUE

EPILOGUE

A time passed.

The rain came weeping down,
softly, like a quiet symphony.
And the insect world came alive;
and out of the earth,
disturbed by the storm,
crawled bugs and beetles,
ants and roaches and spiders.

The rain came down,
and the dust was all now gone.
There seemed a different
atmosphere over the land,
a fresh clean smell in the air,
a new life beginning
for the wet leaves and grass.

And the seeds of corn
in the fields of the land
seemed to awaken of a sudden
in the soft sweet soil.
The corn seeds soon began
to split and push
their miniscule roots
        upwards....
as the rain came down,
gurgling and sighing,
breathing like a thing alive,
        feeding the corn,
giving the corn a life;
soaking into the guts
        of the land,
into the pushing, thrusting

awakening corn,
into the very soul,
the very soul
of
México.

And the dry season
was over....

END